American MuscleCars

American Muscle Cars

JIM CAMPISANO

MetroBooks

An Imprint of Friedman/Fairfax Publishers

Library of Congress Cataloging-in-Publication Data

Campisano, Jim
      American muscle cars / Jim Campisano.
            p. cm.
      Includes bibliographical references and index.
      ISBN 1-56799-164-5
      1. Muscle cars—United States—History. I. Title.
TL23.C36 1995
629.222—dc20   94-34914
                                                                           CIP

Editor: Benjamin Boyington
Art Director: Jeff Batzli
Designer: Kevin Ullrich
Layout Artist: Philip Travisano
Photography Editor: Emilya Naymark

Color separations by Bright Arts (Singapore) Pte. Ltd.
Printed in China by Leefung-Asco Printers, Ltd.

For bulk purchases and special sales, please contact:
Friedman/Fairfax Publishers
Attention: Sales Department
15 West 26th Street
New York, NY 10010
212/685-6610 FAX 212/685-1307

Dedication

For Donna, whose favorite muscle cars are
the Shaft, the Chevrolet Corvair, the Dodge Dart
convertible, and the Nash Metropolitan. Let's cruise.

Acknowledgments

Special thanks to D. Randy Riggs, for mention-
ing my name; Al Kirschenbaum, whose writings in
the 1970s helped steer me to a career of automotive journalism (Al, who actually owned a new
Hemi Dart in 1968 for a couple of weeks, has
been researching Mopar muscle cars for the better
part of three decades and selflessly provided me
with never-before-published Chrysler production
figures. I, and any enthusiast who reads this book,
owe him a huge debt of gratitude); Tom DeMauro,
without whom every word in this book about
Pontiacs would probably be incorrect; Dr. John
Craft, for sharing his knowledge of aero warriors
and for actually using the term "sybaritic accoutrements" in a Boss 302 story; Mike Furman, for his
help with the Oldsmobile parts of this book, especially the W-30 stuff; Donnie Chapman, Jerry
Derise, and Dan Foley, for making my Dodge what
it is today; Jerry Heasley and Ed Cunneen, for their
COPO info; Steve Holly, for his computer know-
how; Michael Breeding and his TBR (nice Buick!);
Mr. Motion himself, Joel Rosen, for offering 11.5-
second Phase III Camaros with money-back guaran-
tees (though I'm still waiting for mine); Jim McCraw,
a real pro, for telling me what it was like at *SS&DI*
in the "good old days"; Bill Bartels, for his appreci-
ation of muscle cars, for letting me drive his '62
Max Wedge Plymouth, and for putting on the
greatest show on earth; Brian Wilson, whose songs
became the soundtrack for every car guy's life; and
anyone who has ever owned, still drives, or loves
muscle cars.

Contents

Introduction

When Brian Wilson wrote "I Get Around" in the early sixties, America was a very different place from what it is today. Hot cars and soft girls were the primary focus of most young men. And while the United States was certainly not the utopia nostalgists would have you believe, it seemed there was no problem that couldn't be solved. The United States had fought back the Germans and the Japanese in the mid-forties, and the recession of the late fifties was over—it was time for a celebration.

What better way to rejoice than by taking a shiny piece of horsepower-laden Detroit iron out on one of Eisenhower's new interstate highways? Chrome, glass, and steel were king, and high-octane gasoline cost about twenty-five cents a gallon. By the 1960 model year, the powers-that-be in Motor City had been engaged in a horsepower war for the better part of a decade. General Motors, Ford, and Chrysler had everything they needed in place for an all-out assault on the streets—including a rapidly expanding audience.

America's legendary love affair with the automobile was rapidly approaching its pinnacle. It would reach that zenith when America's 78 million baby boomers started reaching driving age around 1961. They were young and enthusiastic, and they (or their parents) had an unprecedented amount of discretionary income. Not that it took that much to buy into one of Detroit's dream machines. Long before federal bureaucrats became steeped in every aspect of automobile production, back in the good old days when seat belts could be deleted from your new car for credit and inflation was almost negligible, a brand-spanking-new road rocket could be yours for less than the down payment for an econocar today.

Customers were enthusiastic. When John Z. DeLorean unleashed the 1964 Pontiac GTO on an unsuspecting public, some doubted that it would sell even 5,000 units. When its first-year sales were tallied and it was found that more than six times that many had been sold, all bets were off.

We always take my car 'cause it's never been beat
And we've never missed yet with the girls we meet...
—"I Get Around," by the Beach Boys

(The base price of that same GTO was just over $2,500.) Suddenly, the other divisions at GM, as well as Ford and Chrysler, were scrambling to put modified, large-bore engines in intermediate-size packages.

Of course, the GTO certainly wasn't the first muscle car. What was, you ask? People have argued over this for years. Was it the '49 Rocket 88 from Oldsmobile? Buick's '55 Century Special, which was a high-horsepower Roadmaster engine in the smaller, lighter Special body? The fuel-injected '57 Chevy? The Hemi-powered '55 Chrysler C-300?

Worthy contenders all, but we're going to start in the 1960 model year. For the most part, combinations from before this time had been quickly assembled packages, often utilizing existing hardware. Some, like the Chrysler C-300, were based on full-size, very expensive luxury vehicles. Others, like the dual-quad Chevy Power Packs, offered excellent performance, but lacked the necessary image boosters—bucket seats, floor shifters, and futuristic styling. Back then, most people were not dreaming about the good old days. They were living those dreams, and that meant preparing for a future with unlimited possibilities. The public demanded styling that was lower, longer, and wider, and engines that grew dramatically in size and power each year.

In a way, the muscle car era was a mirror of the sixties. America was a leader, not a follower. It was also a bit of a bully around the globe. The muscle cars reflected this. They were boulevard bruisers, pure and simple. If you didn't have the horsepower, you stayed out of the way. Today, both the American government and the car companies are far more cautious. Rather than going with their instincts, the Big Three now react to what Toyota, Nissan, and Mazda are doing.

But we digress. Muscle cars aren't about sociology. Let the scholars argue about whether the sixties was a better decade than the nineties, whether there's a hole in the ozone, and whether our lust for the internal combustion engine is going to drive mankind to extinction. Muscle cars are about screaming big blocks revving to the redline. They're about full-throttle power-shifts at the drags. They're about crazy colors polished to the max and glittering chrome tailpipes belching smoke and flames. They're about power that pins you to your seat. They're about cruising on a warm summer night with your buddies or that special someone. They are about a bygone era that changed America (and the automobile industry) forever.

While high insurance rates, stricter emissions laws, and expensive fuel helped drive the American muscle cars from the road, they are back today with a vengeance. They are being restored and owned by those who love them most, those who have invested their life savings to preserve the best part of their youth and one of the best parts of American culture.

Climb aboard, buckle up, and prepare for the ride of your life.

For America's baby boomers, muscle cars were freedom wrapped in chrome and steel. With its 425-horsepower engine, the '70 Plymouth Hemicuda (opposite, top) is one of the most fearsome Detroit supercars; it was a direct descendant of the legendary 1956 Chrysler 300B, the first American car to have one horsepower per cubic inch. Long before the Beatles sang of "Revolution," Pontiac's GTO (opposite, bottom: a '66 model) started a revolution of its own by placing a large 389 engine in a midsize body, with just the right amount of sex appeal added for good measure.

Chapter 1

The little old lady from Pasadena

Has a pretty little flower bed of white gardenias

But parked in a rickety old garage

Is a brand-new, shiny red, Super Stock Dodge...

—"The Little Old Lady from Pasadena," by Jan and Dean

Opposite: The roots of the muscle car era are in vehicles like the fuel-injected '57 Chevy Bel Air. Chevrolet offered both the 250- and the 283-horsepower versions of the Corvette's fuel-injected engine in its full-sized cars from 1957 until 1959. Very little on the street could touch them. Above right: The stylish Wide Track Pontiacs of 1959 transformed the division, catapulting it to number three in sales. The 389 V8 used in these cars greatly enhanced performance, both on the street and at the race track.

The 413 Ramcharger. 426 Max Wedge. 348 Police Interceptor. 421 Super Duty. The names themselves are special. Say them over and over again. The effect is hypnotic. They conjure up thoughts of pavement-shredding torque, high-octane fuel, and domination of street and strip. All these engines and many more were available during the first wave of muscle car madness in the early sixties. They were not-so-subtle reminders that the days of the Chevy Stovebolt Six and the Pontiac Torpedo Eight were but a fading memory. And thank goodness for that.

The roots of the supercar era are entrenched in the forties and fifties. Starting in 1949, car manufacturers began introducing powerful, modern, overhead-valve V8 engines. Technological improvements were coming in waves. The buying public's lust for better, more exciting automobiles was at an unprecedented level, and the moguls in Detroit were more than willing to oblige.

The results of this first feeding frenzy were muscle cars that are known today as the factory super stocks. These cars came along about the same time that John F. Kennedy was entering the

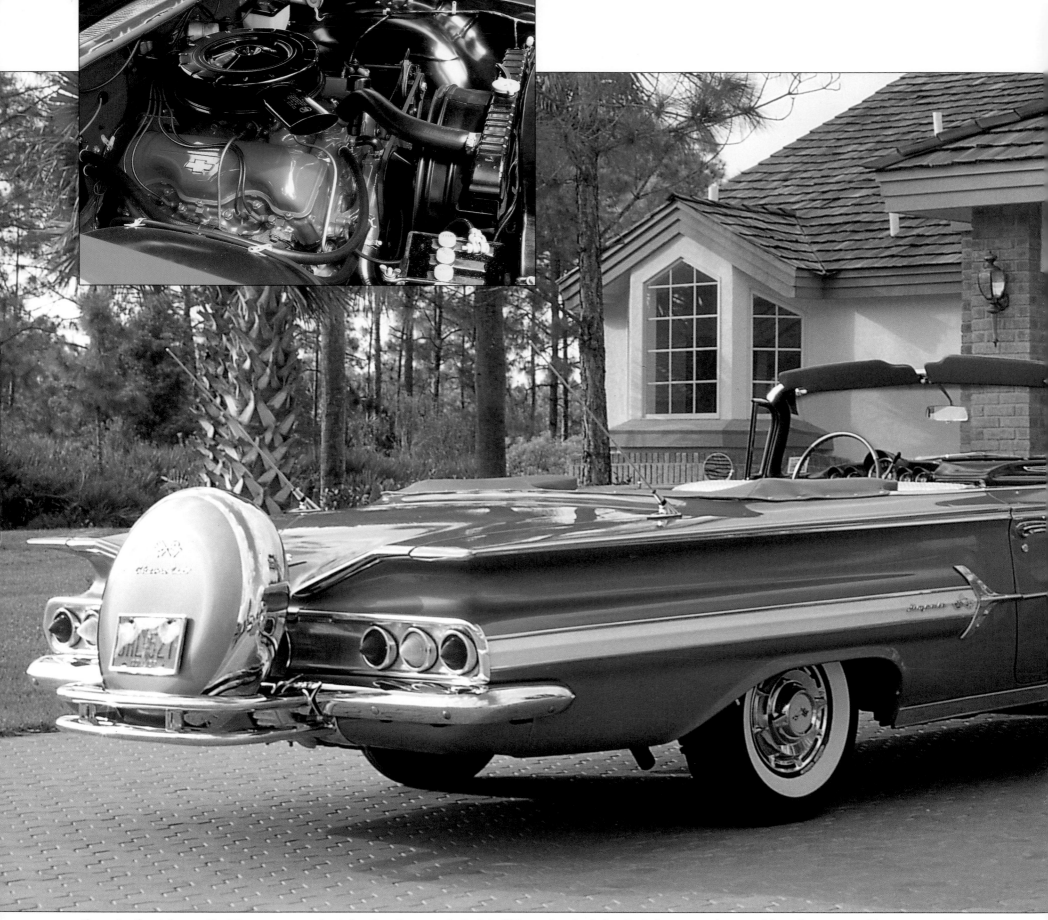

Above: Continental spare tire kits are more popular today than they were in the late fifties and early sixties. Back then, no one interested in performance would put one on a hot car like this 348 Chevy with three-deuce carburetion—it just added weight to a car that was already very heavy. Most Chevrolets received the 348 with the single four-barrel carburetor (inset), which made 320 horsepower.

White House. The prevailing mood in the country was that anything was possible, and Detroit was out to prove that this was true.

Ford vs. Chevy

It should come as little surprise that the age-old brand rivalry between Ford and Chevrolet was at the core of the muscle car wars. Prior to the introduction of the small-block Chevy V8 in 1955, Ford's valve-in-block flathead V8 engine dominated the hot rod scene. While the freshly minted overhead-valve V8s put out by Oldsmobile and Cadillac certainly made plenty of horsepower, they were not readily available in junkyards and were expensively wrapped in virgin sheet metal. The Ford flathead, which was produced from 1932 to 1953, was cheap and plentiful, and was the speed freak's engine of choice in the early days.

When Ford replaced the venerable flathead in 1954, it laid an egg. Among the many problems of the Y-block V8, which superseded the hot-rodders' favorite mill, were a flimsy block and a suspect oiling system. When the 265 small block showed up in the magnificent '55 Chevy, it proved to be the answer to the prayers of enthusiasts everywhere. It was lightweight, high-revving, and long on power. Best of all, it responded to modifications the way a cat does to milk. Where Ford once had a lock on the youth market, Chevy stepped in and took it away—lock, stock, and barrel.

Toward the end of the decade, cars were getting larger and heavier. This led the Big Three to develop hulking, torquier engines to move them. Enter the Chevrolet 348 and the Ford 352 power plants. These engines debuted in 1958 and became primary motivators in the 1960 model year. Eventually, it was Ford that fired the first salvo in the engine wars. Chevrolets were running roughshod over Fords on the street. In situations where the fuel-injected Chevy 283s and dual-quad Power Packs were not enough, the Bowtie brigade could trot out a three-2-barrel version of the 348 (the progenitor of the soon-to-be-legendary 409) in a stylish Impala.

In 1960 Ford introduced the 352 Special, which was engineered from the bottom up to be an all-out performer. It was based on the big-block FE design. Its compression ratio was raised from 10.2:1 to 10.6:1. The engineers added stronger connecting rods, flattop pistons, a 60-psi oil pump, and stouter bearings. The cylinder heads had smaller combustion chambers (hence the higher compression ratio), but the real keys were the camshaft and the intake and exhaust manifolds.

Opening and closing the valves was a 306-degree solid-lifter cam with 0.480-inch valve lift—radical for 1960. Induction chores were handled by a Holley 550 cfm 4-barrel carb on an aluminum intake (topped by an open-element air cleaner), while exhaust gases were carried away by a set of low-restriction split-flow exhaust manifolds.

Ford rated the 352 Special at a robust 360 horsepower at 6000 rpm, 60 more ponies than standard. The two big drawbacks to the package were weak, soft valve springs (on early versions) and the transmission—a 3-speed manual shift mounted on the column.

Fortunately, Ford could put the 352 Special in an attractive, all-new body. The '60 full-size Ford was redesigned from the ground up, and was low, wide, and sleek.

Chevy's big gun was the 348 Police Interceptor, also known as the W-motor because of the shape of its cylinder heads. For this engine, the designers placed the intake and exhaust valves closer to their respective ports. Because of the W shape, the spark plugs could be quite close to the center of the combustion chamber.

Not long after it hit the market in 1958, the 348 sported three Rochester 2-barrel carbs on an iron intake. It was good for 280 horses and, more importantly, 370 lbs.-ft. of torque. Not bad for a first-year mill. By 1960 it had been refined and enhanced. Horsepower was up to 335 at 5800 rpm. It featured 11.25:1 compression, dual exhausts, and its own version of the famed Duntov camshaft—named for its designer, Belgian-born Zora Arkus-Duntov, who is more widely known today as the godfather of the Corvette.

While the Ford big block had more horsepower on paper, the Chevy motor was more of a force to be reckoned with, thanks to its Warner T-10 4-speed manual gearbox. In a stripped-down Bel Air, the three-deuce 348 would be good for mid- to high 15-second elapsed times (ETs) at about 90 mph. A 352 Ford was at best a 15.9-second machine on the stock tires.

A fifteen-year war had begun.

The Competition

You can sell an old man a young man's car, but you can't sell a young man an old man's car.

—Semon E. "Bunkie" Knudsen

Fortunately for car enthusiasts, Chrysler and General Motors' other divisions were also playing the muscle car game. Pontiac was every bit as interested in performance as Ford and Chevy, perhaps even more so.

Prior to 1958, Pontiac's image was the stodgiest in the industry. The typical Pontiac was the perfect car for someone's grandmother. When Semon E. "Bunkie" Knudsen took over the division in 1956, his first priority was to inject some life into the lineup. The first thing he did was remove the Indian-head emblem and the chrome "suspenders" (as he called them) that ran the length of the hood on Pontiac cars. He associated them with the division's dowdy image. When Knudsen's first Wide Track models hit the showrooms three years later, they created a sensation. Sales skyrocketed and it wasn't long before Pontiac became the third-best-selling nameplate in the country.

Pontiac's new role as a sportier, young man's car (which it continues to play up today) was based on futuristic styling and "right-now" performance. As he reinvented Pontiac, Knudsen increased its presence in NASCAR (the National Association for Stock Car Auto Racing) and drag racing. Its first entry into the street skirmish was the 1960 Trophy 425-A engine.

PONTIAC

1960

Cu. In.	389
Bore (in.)	4.06
Stroke (in.)	3.75
Compression	10.75:1
Induction	3x2 bbl.
Horsepower/RPM	348/4800
Torque (lbs.-ft.)/RPM	425/2800

1961

Cu. In.	389		421
Bore (in.)	4.06		4.09
Stroke (in.)	3.75		4.00
Compression	10.75:1		11.00:1
Induction	1x4 bbl.	3x2 bbl.	2x4 bbl.
Horsepower/RPM	333/4800	348/4800	373*/5600
Torque (lbs.-ft.)/RPM	425/2800	430/2800	not rated

*Over-the-counter option only

1962

Cu. In.	389		
Bore (in.)	4.06		
Stroke (in.)	3.75		
Compression	10.75:1		
Induction	1x4 bbl.	3x2 bbl.	1x4 bbl.*
Horsepower/RPM	333/4800	348/4800	385/5200
Torque (lbs.-ft.)/RPM	425/2800	430/2800	430/3200

*Super Duty option

1962 (cont.)

Cu. In.	421*
Bore (in.)	4.09
Stroke (in.)	4.00
Compression	11.00:1
Induction	2x4 bbl.
Horsepower/RPM	405/5600
Torque (lbs.-ft.)/RPM	425/4400

*Super Duty option

1963

Cu. In.	421		
Bore (in.)	4.09		
Stroke (in.)	4.00		
Compression	10.75:1		12.00:1*
Induction	1x4 bbl.	3x2 bbl.	1x4 bbl.
Horsepower/RPM	353/5000	370/5200	390/5800
Torque (lbs.-ft.)/RPM	455/3400	460/3800	425/3600

*Super Duty option

1963 (cont.)

Cu. In.	421*	
Bore (in.)	4.09	
Stroke (in.)	4.00	
Compression	12.00:1	13.00:1*
Induction	2x4 bbl.	2x4 bbl.
Horsepower/RPM	405/5600	410/5600
Torque (lbs.-ft.)/RPM	425/4400	435/4400

*Super Duty option

The Wide-Track styling introduced on the '59 Pontiac set the market on fire and evolved by 1962 into, among other things, the breathtaking '62 Pontiac Grand Prix. This example is one of the rare 15 built with the for-racers-only 421 Super Duty engine.

Plymouths were hamstrung by styling that, charitably, could best be described as weird—even by garish 1950s standards.

The Mopar (Chrysler) engineers, however, were busy developing the 383 B-engine and the raised block (RB) 413—both of which would soon be mainstays of the muscle car era. At the same time, they introduced the most bizarre induction system ever seen on production vehicles, before or since.

For 1960 both Dodge and Plymouth offered the 383 Long Ram engine, the name of which was derived from its extremely unusual induction setup. The Long Ram featured a pair of Carter carburetors, each sitting at the end of a crisscrossing manifold. Each of these carburetors fed the cylinders on the opposite side of the engine, resulting in intake runner lengths of about 30 inches, and the carbs rested over the valve covers. This setup was designed to bounce suction waves on each intake stroke and thus produce a supercharging effect at mid-range speeds.

The designation for the Trophy engine came from its 425 lbs.-ft. torque rating, not its cubic inch displacement. It had a 389-cube block and boasted a 10.75:1 compression ratio, 4-bolt main caps, Tri-Power carburetion, a split duration camshaft, and free-flowing exhaust manifolds feeding dual exhaust, or twice pipes. Horsepower was 348 at 4800 rpm.

The 389 turned out to be an excellent street engine, making gobs of torque throughout the rpm range. In the stylish Catalina body, it was a true brawler on Main Street, especially with a Warner T-10 4-speed. Although the 389 was garnering quite a reputation for itself on the tracks (Pontiac won seven NASCAR races in 1960, thirty in 1961, and twenty-two in 1962), its status was not cast in bronze until it was wrapped in GTO sheet metal in 1964.

Chrysler, meanwhile, took its time finding its way. While its early Hemi engines were stout performers and its '55 C-300 boasted 300 horsepower, these Chrysler products never caught on with younger buyers. The letter-series Chryslers were very expensive, and the Dodges and

The 1960 Plymouths were heavier than the competition, but the Long Ram intake runners gave the 383 (top) added torque. Manufacturers today still look back to these designs for inspiration. As Chrysler engineers discovered in the fifties, horsepower and torque can be increased by varying intake manifold runner length. Unlike the compact cars that would bear the name in the mid-sixties, the '60 Dart D-500 (above) was a massive automobile with outrageous styling. When fitted with the 383 Long Ram V8, it made for a slick highway cruiser, but not much of a threat at the drag strip.

Somehow, it actually worked. Output for the raised-block 383 was 340 horsepower at 5000 rpm and an earthshaking 460 lbs.-ft. at 2800 rpm. Chrysler engineers had experimented with different runner lengths, and had found out that the torque peak could be varied by shortening or lengthening the runners. This information would become very important very quickly by 1962.

"She's Real Fine, My 409"

At the time of its introduction in 1961, the 409 was a mere blip on the screen. It was fast, yes, but almost an aberration. Only 142 were made and many showed up in the hands of racers. But by the end of the model year, everyone knew about it.

Long before the Beach Boys popularized it, the "4-speed, dual quad, Positraction 409" was tearing it up at drag strips across the country. By giving the 348 a bigger bore and a longer stroke, Chevrolet engineers unleashed the hottest engine

The 1962 "bubble top" Bel Airs (above left) are among the most sought-after first-generation muscle cars. This one sports the 409-hp 409 engine (above right). The twelve cars equipped for racing with aluminum front ends are worth their weight in gold. For 1963 Chevy's designers moved away from the bubble top styling; the '63 Impala SS (left) featured a more formal roofline.

yet on the American public. News of its coming spread rapidly, thanks to its success on the NASCAR speedways (twelve victories) and in the hands of drag racers like "Dyno" Don Nicholson and Dave Strickler.

In street trim, the 409 sported a new aluminum "dual-plane" intake manifold and the brand-new 650 cfm Carter AFB 4-barrel carb (the largest available at the time). The single 4-throat 409 carried a horsepower rating of 360 at 5800 rpm and 409 lbs.-ft. of torque at 3600 rpm. Stuffed into the sleek new Impala body, it pushed elapsed times to the brink of the 14-second barrier in pure stock trim.

A lot could be said for the new '61 Chevys. They were entirely brand-new and had left behind all of the fifties' design cliches. While it was also available as a coupe, the "bubble top" fastback Impala was a remarkable-looking car, then and now.

The full impact of the 409 on the street was a year or so away, but the mighty 348 Police Interceptor was still available for the masses, now with 350 horsepower. Actually, you could bill 1961 as a year of growth and transition. Most of the strongest power plants were available only in limited numbers or were very expensive.

While Chevy introduced its new engine, Ford upped the ante on its 352. By boring it out .050 inch and increasing its stroke from 3.50 inches to 3.78, Ford converted the 352 into the 390, a staple of the Ford performance camp until

These cutaway drawings of the '61 409 show many of its design features. As seen from the top photo, the block's deck surface is 74 degrees off the cylinder centerline, as opposed to 90 degrees on a typical V8. In the bottom photo, you can see the unconventional W-shape of the cylinder head and the effect it had on the placement of the valves. Because of this unique arrangement, the engineers could better place the spark plugs for quicker burn and reduced oil fouling. The plugs were situated above the exhaust manifolds.

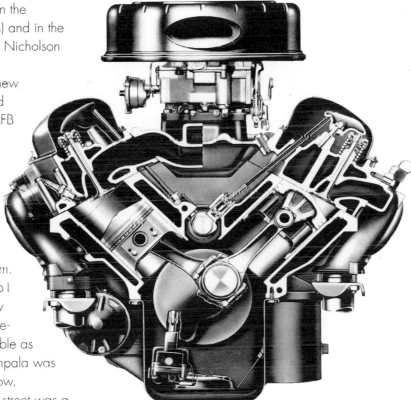

CHEVROLET

1960

Cu. In.	348	
Bore (in.)	4.13	
Stroke (in.)	3.25	
Compression	11.25:1	
Induction	1x4 bbl.	3x2 bbl.
Horsepower/RPM	320/5600	335/5600
Torque (lbs.-ft.)/RPM	358/3600	362/3600

1961

Cu. In.	348		409
Bore (in.)	4.13		4.31
Stroke (in.)	3.25		3.50
Compression	11.25:1		11.00:1
Induction	1x4 bbl.	3x2 bbl.	1x4 bbl.
Horsepower/RPM	340/5800	350/6000	360/5800
Torque (lbs.-ft.)/RPM	362/3600	364/3600	409/3600

1962

Cu. In.	409	
Bore (in.)	4.31	
Stroke (in.)	3.50	
Compression	11.00:1	
Induction	1x4 bbl.	2x4 bbl.
Horsepower/RPM	380/5800	409/6000
Torque (lbs.-ft.)/RPM	420/3200	420/4000

1963

Cu. In.	409		
Bore (in.)	4.31		
Stroke (in.)	3.50		
Compression	10.00:1	11.00:1	
Induction	1x4 bbl.	1x4 bbl.	2x4 bbl.
Horsepower/RPM	340/5000	400/5800	425/6000
Torque (lbs.-ft.)/RPM	420/3200	425/3200	425/4000

Super Duty Legend and Lore

It's hard to imagine today, but Pontiacs were once the car of choice for professional racers. This was due in no small part to the success of the Super Duty parts program.

After June 6, 1957, when the Automobile Manufacturers Association (an organization made up of representatives from Ford, General Motors, and Chrysler) voted to ban their own active participation in auto racing, Bunkie Knudsen and Pontiac chief engineer Pete Estes tried to find a way around the AMA edict. Knudsen was certain that participation in racing was critical to Pontiac's fortunes.

What they did was begin development of parts (and later, cars) that would be sold over the counter "for off road use only" on the 389. From 1959 to 1961, Pontiacs really began to rip things up at the drag strips and on NASCAR's speedways. Most notable was the stellar combination of driver Fireball Roberts and mechanic Smokey Yunick—they won more stock car races over that three-year period than anyone else. Pontiac's thirty victories in 1961, in fact, constitute a record that has been matched only once—by Ford in 1964—and surpassed only by Ford's forty-eight victories in 1965.

One of the top developments of the Super Duty program was the cylinder heads that would end up on the 421 SD in 1962. They had much larger ports and bigger valves than standard 389 heads. For drag racing, the 421 Super Dutys had dual Carter 4-barrels for improved breathing (NASCAR limited all cars to one 4-barrel). Pontiac rated the 2x4 421 at 405 horsepower at 5600 rpm.

Meanwhile, engineer Mac McKellar was designing a series of outstanding camshafts (both the NHRA [National Hot Rod Association] and NASCAR required stock cams).

For 1962 Pontiac built a number of Super Duty Catalinas. They had aluminum front ends (including bumpers), which saved over 200 pounds for drag racing. They came without sound-deadening material and with aluminum exhaust manifolds. (NASCAR versions got stamped-steel headers because the aluminum versions would melt with extended use.) Another odd fact is that Pontiac built fif-

Besides being one of the snazziest cars of the sixties, the '62 Super Duty Pontiac was one of the period's most potent performers. For NASCAR racing, this car was limited to a single 4-barrel carburetor and endowed with cast iron exhaust manifolds. The SD pictured above was built for the drags and sports 2x4 carburetion and 405 rated horsepower (below right). In a road test, *Motor Trend* magazine clocked a 421 Super Duty at 13.9 seconds at 107 mph in the quarter-mile.

teen Super Duty Grand Prixs in 1962, only one of which is known to exist today.

In 1963 the Super Dutys got a new cam, modified cylinder heads with bigger valves, and an increase in compression from 11:1 to 12:1 and 13:1. Dual valve springs were used to increase redline from 6000 to 6400 rpm. Despite all the added goodies, Pontiac raised horsepower only slightly—to 390 for a single 4-barrel with 12:1, 405 with two 4-barrels and 12:1, and 410 with dual quads and 13:1 squeeze.

The Super Dutys were lightened even further with the incorporation of Plexiglas side windows and aluminum trunklids, bellhousing, tailshaft, and rear-axle center section. Finally, Pontiac engineers showed how serious they were about speed by drilling lightening holes into the frame rails. These vehicles were so riddled with holes that they became known as "Swiss Cheese" cars.

Despite the success of the Super Dutys, GM's corporate honchos clamped down on all racing activity in 1963 and the Super Duty program died a rather untimely death.

DODGE/PLYMOUTH

1960

Cu. In.	383
Bore (in.)	4.25
Stroke (in.)	3.38
Compression	10.00:1
Induction	2x4 bbl.
Horsepower/RPM	340/5000
Torque (lbs.-ft.)/RPM	460/2800

1961

Cu. In.	383		413
Bore (in.)	4.25		4.18
Stroke (in.)	3.38		3.75
Compression	10.00:1		10.00:1
Induction	1x4 bbl.	2x4 bbl.	2x4 bbl.
Horsepower/RPM	325/4600	340/5000	375/5000
Torque (lbs.-ft.)/RPM	425/2800	460/2800	465/2800

1962

Cu. In.	413	
Bore (in.)	4.19	
Stroke (in.)	3.75	
Compression	11.00:1	13.51:1
Induction	2x4 bbl.	2x4 bbl.
Horsepower/RPM	410/5400	420/5400
Torque (lbs.-ft.)/RPM	460/4400	460/4400

1963

Cu. In.	426	
Bore (in.)	4.25	
Stroke (in.)	3.75	
Compression	11.00:1	13.51:1
Induction	2x4 bbl.	2x4 bbl.
Horsepower/RPM	415/5600	425/5600
Torque (lbs.-ft.)/RPM	470/4400	480/4400

For 1963 the Plymouth Savoy was restyled, making it more popular with the buying public, and given a 426 cube version of the Max Wedge V8, which made it a favorite of Mopar racers and the bane of the competition. Even with 11:1 compression, this car could run high 12-second quarter-mile ETs when equipped with racing slicks.

1969. Engineers beefed up the bottom end for reliability and horsepower was pegged at 375 at 6000 rpm.

Then Ford announced that it would be fitting the larger FE with wild 6-barrel carburetion. It offered three Holley 2-barrel carbs on an aluminum dual-plane intake. This called for a horsepower rating of 401—more than one horse per cubic inch. Like the 409, however, few 390-6V engines made it down the assembly line. Most were installed by dealers.

One other bit of good news for Ford fanciers was the introduction of the T-10 4-speed manual transmission in April 1961. Similar to the tranny installed in GM's muscle cars, the T-10 4-speed had a wider gearset for better acceleration.

For Mopar fanatics, Chrysler introduced the 413 Long Ram engine in Dodges and Plymouths. Because of their special-order status, delivery times for the 413 Long Rams were lengthy, and many buyers settled for 383 models.

While everyone else was dabbling in exotic induction and bigger-bore mills, Pontiac was busy churning out actual cars. Its 425-A Trophy V8 was basically a carryover, but it was being sold in increasing numbers. Its performance image was expanding rapidly.

There is more to the Pontiac story, however, than just its street engines.

Introducing Max Wedge

Max Wedge was the name given by racers, enthusiasts, and the press to the dominant 413 Mopar engines of 1962. Packed into the new downsized Dodge and Plymouth bodies, these engines resulted

While the styling of the '62 and '63 Dodges (left and above, respectively) never won any prizes, these cars finished first in the quarter-mile more often than not. In 1963 the Dodge raced by the Ramchargers race team took the Stock class championship at the Winternationals with a 12.44/115 mph ET.

in all out race cars designed for street use. While Chrysler may have come to the party late, its arrival signaled the beginning of a new era.

How did the Mopars go from also rans to kings of the hill seemingly overnight? It took equal doses of engineering brilliance, mega horsepower, and decision making that was (truth be told) all wrong.

Chrysler's technological might was never in question, and years of development made its 413 one of the strongest power plants around. The secret to its muscle car success in 1962 was a misjudgment on the part of the executives about where the market was headed. Believing that consumers wanted smaller cars, the executives at Chrysler prepared to build them. For 1962 Chrysler scaled down its cars to what was considered midsize proportions then. As a result of this size change, as well as styling that was again controversial, Chrysler took it on the chin saleswise.

But for racers, smaller is always better—smaller means lighter—and Mopar engineers gave them another advantage when they also introduced unitized construction on these B-body cars this year, cutting even more weight. This meant that you could get the most powerful engines Mother Mopar could dream up in automobiles that were roughly 300 to 500 pounds lighter than the competition.

In 1962 there were two 413 Max Wedges available (in the Dodge this engine was called the 413 Ramcharger; in the Plymouth it was called the 413 Super Stock). They shared many of the same components, including forged-aluminum TRW pistons, a hardened crank, and beefier rods. Both got a 300-degree solid-lifter camshaft with heavy-duty springs, big-port heads, and dual Carter AFBs on a short ram intake manifold (15-inch runners). The standard rear was Mopar's near-indestructible 8¾-inch unit. All had 3.91 gears with Sure-Grip, though other ratios were available as a dealer-installed option.

Max Wedge Mopars also shared special exhaust manifolds. Made of heavy cast iron, these headers ran into 3-inch-diameter pipes featuring dump tubes that could be opened for competition in less than five minutes. If there was any doubt that Detroit was building race cars for the street, these Dodges and Plymouths put it to rest.

The more "streetable" of the engines sported 11:1 compression and was rated at 410 horsepower at 5400 rpm, while the other had 13.5:1 compression and 420 horsepower at 5400 rpm. Neither was for the fainthearted, but the latter mill really could be considered only for a race vehicle.

For shift-it-yourselfers, a heavy-duty T-85 3-speed manual was available, but the hot ticket was Chrysler's TorqueFlite 3-speed automatic, which came beefed up from the factory. It was the first automatic that could shift quicker and harder than a stick.

The downside was that the Mopars were built in extremely limited numbers. Only two hundred were initially planned, and while demand pushed

Old Reliable—Dave Strickler

The shifts came so quickly and so smoothly that those watching argued whether the car was a 4-speed or an automatic. The virgin white Chevy with "The Old Reliable" script on the side was a terror from coast to coast, due in large part to the young man behind the wheel. His name was Dave Ziegler Strickler and he handled the Hurst shifter of his 4-speed gearbox with the same deftness Michelangelo had reserved for a paintbrush.

A native of York, Pennsylvania, Strickler began racing Chevys in 1959 with a 348-powered Biscayne. And he did so successfully. One day, the W-motor was running a bit poorly and he mentioned it to the steward at Lancaster Speedway. The steward turned out to be none other than Bill "Grumpy" Jenkins, who adjusted the tuning of the motor so that the car ran better that it had before. Soon the pair had teamed up on a series of Chevys and then, after the GM racing ban, a Dodge. The results were a rewrite of the record books and an eventual spot in the NHRA's Northeast Division Drag Racing Hall of Fame.

In 1960 Strickler again campaigned a Biscayne coupe. Again, he did quite well. When the budget got strained, he worked out a sponsorship deal with Ammon R. Smith Chevrolet in his hometown for the 1961 season. The result of that deal was a 409 Biscayne, the first car to sport "The Old Reliable" logo, which was the dealership's motto. Records fell, and Strickler and Jenkins began match racing the Chevy around the country.

For 1962 Strickler and Jenkins took delivery of a 409-horse 409 bubble top Bel Air, a.k.a. Old Reliable II. They racked up almost 150,000 miles traversing the United States, winning races and toppling performance benchmarks along the way.

Old Reliable III was one of the ultrarare Z-11 aluminum front end Impalas, which put it in the B/Factory Experimental class, but it was Old Reliable IV that created the most commotion. It had the lightweight sheet metal like III, but the special Z-11 427-cubic-inch version of the W-motor, a 4-speed transmission, vented metallic brakes, a special cowl, an induction air cleaner, and a Positraction axle. The sound deadener was deleted, as was the front sway bar. By the end of the season, the Jenkins-prepped missile had won about 90 percent of the two hundred races it ran.

General Motors' racing ban in 1963 sent Strickler and Jenkins to the Mopar camp in 1964. Dodge provided factory support in the form of a Max Wedge hardtop and two lightweight Hemi sedans. Finally, in 1965, the team split up when Jenkins got his own ride, the Plymouth "Black Arrow." Strickler's factory ride was one of the six almighty altered-wheel-base, lightweight Dodge Coronet Hemis.

By 1966 Strickler was back driving Chevrolets, and he stuck with them throughout the decade. He even teamed up with Jenkins in 1969 and 1970 to produce a series of performance seminars and youth auto safety clinics at Chevrolet dealerships.

The desire to spend more time with his family played a large part in Strickler's decision to retire after the 1974 season. Sadly, time was not on his side—he died of a massive heart attack on June 6, 1985, while mowing his lawn in York. He was just forty-four years old.

Dave Strickler takes off in Old Reliable II, the second of his Ammon R. Smith Chevrolet–sponsored Super Stocks, at New Jersey's now-defunct Vineland Speedway.

FORD

1960

Cu. In.	352
Bore (in.)	4.00
Stroke (in.)	3.50
Compression	10.60:1
Induction	1x4 bbl.
Horsepower/RPM	360/6000
Torque (lbs.-ft.)/RPM	380/3400

1961

Cu. In.	390	
Bore (in.)	4.05	
Stroke (in.)	3.78	
Compression	10.60:1	
Induction	1x4 bbl.	3x2 bbl.
Horsepower/RPM	375/6000	401/6000
Torque (lbs.-ft.)/RPM	427/3400	430/3500

1962

Cu. In.	390	406	
Bore (in.)	4.05	4.13	
Stroke (in.)	3.78	3.78	
Compression	10.50:1	11.40:1	
Induction	1x4 bbl.	1x4 bbl.	3x2 bbl.
Horsepower/RPM	340/5000	385/5800	405/5800
Torque (lbs.-ft.)/RPM	430/3200	444/3400	448/3500

1963

Cu. In.	390	406	
Bore (in.)	4.05	4.13	
Stroke (in.)	3.78	3.78	
Compression	10.50:1	11.40:1	
Induction	1x4 bbl.	1x4 bbl.	3x2 bbl.
Horsepower/RPM	330/5000	385/5800	405/5800
Torque (lbs.-ft.)/RPM	427/3200	444/3400	448/3500

1963 (cont.)

Cu. In.	427	
Bore (in.)	4.23	
Stroke (in.)	3.78	
Compression	11.00:1	
Induction	1x4 bbl.	2x4 bbl.
Horsepower/RPM	410/5600	425/6000
Torque (lbs.-ft.)/RPM	476/3400	480/3700

Despite having up to 405 horsepower available, the '62 Ford (above) never caught on with the street racing crowd. It also did poorly in stock car racing, winning only six races to Pontiac's twenty-two and Chevrolet's fourteen. For $379.70, you got the 406 (right) with 3×2 carburetion, heavy-duty suspension and brakes, and a 4-speed transmission, among other things.

that number to three hundred (split almost equally between Dodge and Plymouth models), these cars were hardly plentiful on the street. Production of the 409 Chevy was now going full tilt and the 409 could be had with two 4-barrel carbs (409 hp). Ford again increased displacement of the FE motor, this time to 406 cubic inches, and the FE became available with three 2-barrels (and bigger exhaust valves) for 405 hp.

Thanks to the exploits of drag racers like Don Nicholson, Hayden Profitt, and Dave Strickler, the 409 was the most sought-after muscle car in 1962. It was available in any full-size Chevy, including wagons, and could be had with either a 3-speed or 4-speed manual transmission with floor shifter. (No automatics were vailable.)

The two 650 cfm Carters were on a new aluminum dual-plane intake, and the new cylinder heads had ¼-inch higher intake ports. Intake valve diameter increased from 2.07 to 2.20 inches. This

gave the W-motor much better breathing. Horsepower for the new engine was 409 at 6000 revs. It was good for mid-14s at close to 98 mph off the showroom floor.

How Big Does This Thing Get?

When Ford engineers bored out the 390 from 4.05 inches to 4.13 in 1962, they broke the 400-cubic-inch barrier by 6 inches. A complete 406 package cost $379.70, and you really got a lot for your money: three-deuce carburetion, heavy-duty suspension and brakes, a 4-speed trans with heavy-duty clutch, and an upgraded cooling system, among other things. Certainly, all the hardware was there.

While the United States and the Soviet Union were engaged in an all-out arms race, the Big Three were holding a race of their own. In only a couple of short years, cubic inches had climbed from around 350 or so to well over 400. And there seemed to be no limit to how far the automakers would go in their quest for road and track supremacy. That's why both NASCAR and the NHRA imposed a 7.0-liter (427.5 cubes) limit for engine size in 1963.

To take full advantage of this, some of the top motors were pushed to this limit. Ford's 406 became the 427, the 413 Max Wedge became the 426, and Chevrolet introduced a 427-cubic-inch version of its 409 for competition. Pontiac stayed put with the 421.

The theme of Ford's ad campaign in 1963 was "Total Performance," and there could be no question that the gang from Dearborn had it. The 427 not only was bigger than the 406 (thanks to its increase in bore from 4.13 to 4.23), but also had improved cylinder heads and available dual 550 cfm Holleys on an aluminum intake manifold.

When placed in a car like the lightweight Galaxie, the 427 engine (above) put Ford back in the winner's circle, both at the drags and on NASCAR's high banks. Ford's NASCAR efforts were bolstered by the midyear 1963 introduction of the Galaxie fastback (right), the aerodynamics of which greatly increased top speed.

This was rated at 425 horsepower at 6000 rpm, while a single 4-barrel was standard with 410.

By midyear, the big Ford looked as strong as it went. A fastback version of the Galaxie—perhaps the prettiest postwar Blue Oval—came along in '63½ and was aerodynamic enough to make Ford a force on NASCAR's super speedways. With Tiny Lund behind the wheel and the 427 under the hood, a Ford won the Daytona 500.

Following the introduction of the fastback in 1963, Ford built fifty-five lightweight Galaxie race cars equipped with dual-quad 427s. The doors, hood, trunklids, and other front-end pieces were fiberglass, while the bumpers and 4-speed transmission cases were made of aluminum. All superfluous amenities and parts were deleted.

This was also the year that Mercury fans got in on some of the muscle car fun. The S-55 Marauder was offered in either single or dual 4-barrel trim (called the Super Marauder). With Parnelli Jones behind the wheel, an S-55 captured the Pikes Peak Hill Climb in 1963 and 1964. These un-Mercury-like engines were available until 1966, when they were replaced by the 428.

In 1963 Chevrolet was kind enough to add better cylinder heads and a hotter camshaft to the 409, giving it a horsepower rating equal to that of Ford's dual-quad engine. There was even a 340-horse version offered with hydraulic lifters and a softer camshaft. Most people's curiosity, however, was piqued by the Z-11 competition package. Designed for drag racing, this package included a 427 (enlarged from a 409), and aluminum front sheet metal and bumpers (to save 112 pounds). Many of the front brackets and much of the bracing were deleted.

The engine sported 13.5:1 compression and was rated at 430 horsepower at 5800 revs and 430 lbs.-ft. of torque at 4200 rpm. Only fifty-five were ever built (or fifty-seven, depending on who you believe), and at $1,245 the Z-11 was the most expensive regular production option ever offered in a Chevy. To get one, you had to be someone special and have friends in high places. Those who didn't could buy the lightweight fenders and hoods over the counter.

While Ford and Chevrolet were busying themselves trying to dominate race tracks, Pontiac's John

Pontiac put most of its Super Duty engines in 1962 Catalinas like the one pictured above. Much rarer were the fifteen Super Duty Grand Prixs built that year—only one of these is known to exist today.

DeLorean and Pete Estes were coming up with a superpotent street version of the 421. Called the 421 H.O., it had 10.75:1 compression, 1.92/1.66-inch valve heads, Tri-Power, a 292/302-degree hydraulic cam, and new exhaust manifolds. With 370 hp at 5200 rpm, it was a worthy successor to the Trophy 389s and a real force on the boulevard. There was also a single 4-barrel version rated at 353 horses.

The only bad news for General Motors fans in 1963 was the front-office edict banning all divisions from participating in racing activities. This dealt a crushing blow to a multitude of programs, including the Z-11 Chevys, Pontiac Super Dutys, and Corvette Grand Sports, which were trying desperately to catch up with the great Carroll Shelby's Cobras.

As a result of dismal sales in 1962, Chrysler revamped the lineups of both its Dodge and Plymouth divisions in 1963. Styling was toned down, but it still wasn't what you would call conventional. The Dart moniker was switched to

Dodge's compact car and its midsize cars were all completely remodeled. The hot 426 Ramcharger V8 was installed in what was now called the 330—a real stripped-down model—the 440, and the more upscale Polara and Polara 500. Plymouth kept wheelbases at 116 inches, while Dodge stretched them to 119.

Looks were of little importance to racers and Mopar enthusiasts. All that mattered were elapsed times. Thanks to an increased bore and displacement, power in the Max Wedge was quoted at 415 ponies at 5600 rpm and 470 lbs.-ft. of torque at 4400, with 11:1 compression and 425 hp and 480 lbs.-ft. at the same rpm with 13.5:1 squeeze. Contrary to what has been published elsewhere, the engine, including the intake and carbs, was basically a carryover. The biggest changes were slightly larger ports in the heads and an upgraded oiling system.

On July 23, however, things changed dramatically—Chrysler announced the introduction of its Stage II Max Wedge. According to automotive

journalist and Mopar historian Al Kirschenbaum, heads, cam, springs, carbs, and other essential parts were upgraded to bring the 426 up to Stage II specs (though official horsepower ratings stayed the same).

Changes to the heads included further relief machining in the combustion chambers around the intake valves, while undervalve bowl areas in the inlet passage were enlarged and relieved to improve mixture flow. A new cam gave more lift and increased duration, and new Carter carbs had more venturi area.

For the truly hardcore, aluminum front end panels became available in 1963. The package included fenders, fresh-air scooped hood, splash shields, and aluminum bumper brackets, as well as other minor pieces. All Mopars so equipped came from the factory with trunk-mounted batteries—in fact, they were the only Max Wedges with factory trunk-mounted batteries. Chrysler probably never sold even a hundred of these lightweight vehicles, but it still managed to skirt the requirements of the

Ten Quickest Muscle Cars, 1960–1963

1. 1963 Dodge/Plymouth 426 Max Wedge
2. 1962 Dodge/Plymouth 413 Max Wedge
3. 1962–1963 Corvette 327/365 F.I.
4. 1963 Chevy Bel Air 409/425 hp
5. 1963 Ford Galaxie 427/425 hp
6. 1962 Chevy Bel Air 409/409 hp
7. 1963 Pontiac Catalina 421 H.O.
8. 1962 Ford Galaxie 406/405 hp
9. 1961 Chevy 409/380 hp
10. 1961 Chevy 348/335 hp

Some readers may disagree with some of these ratings. Certainly, Pontiac fans will wonder where the Super Dutys are. But the early SDs were really out-and-out race cars. You had to be a licensed NHRA drag racer to buy one. Depending on the driver, a '62 or '63 327 fuel-injected 'Vette with a 4-speed and 4.11 or 4.56 gears would run right past a 409 Chevy and be highly competitive with a 413 Mopar.

sanctioning bodies with a good paper shuffle and retrofitting of parts.

The year 1963 marked the last great stand of the factory super stocks. When Pontiac introduced the GTO in 1964, the days of big-car performance were numbered. Only a fool, however, would underrate these behemoths. Truth be told, many of these early Goats were a step down in the performance department.

Not long after the '64 GTOs hit the showrooms, President John F. Kennedy was assassinated. While the two events are obviously unrelated, neither America nor the car-buying public would ever be the same again. A new age was dawning.

While the '62 Corvette (top) sported only 327 cubes, it could run faster than most, thanks to its 365-horsepower fuel-injected engine, 1,000-lb. weight advantage, and available axle ratios up to 4.56:1 from the factory. Thanks to a 13.5:1 compression engine and dual quads, the '63 426 Max Wedge Plymouths (middle) and Dodges were the quickest of the early muscle machines. The '61 348 Impala (bottom)—a serious player on the street—gave rise to the 409.

Chapter 2

1964–1967: America Gets Its Goat— and a Whole Lot More

*Little GTO, you're really
  lookin' fine
Three deuces and a
  4-speed and a 389
Listen to her taching
  up now
Listen to her whine
Come on and turn it on,
  wind it up, blow it
  out GTO...*

—"Little GTO," by Ronnie & the

Daytonas

The potent 427 Ford Galaxie (above right) was one of the top performers of 1964, but the success of the 389-powered Pontiac GTO (introduced that same year) spelled doom for fullsize muscle cars. Pontiac's "Goat" spawned a host of imitators over the years, one of the finest being the 1967 Plymouth GTX (opposite), which was powered by a 375-horse 440.

General Motors' corporate racing ban did more than just bring to an abrupt halt the research and development on some very important projects. All of a sudden, Chevrolet and Pontiac had no way to promote their growing lineup of high-performance vehicles and parts.

Then an idea sprang from the fertile mind of Pontiac general manager John Zachary DeLorean—a notion so simple, yet so brilliant. Why not take a warmed-over big-car engine—one that would idle in traffic and would not overheat in the summer—and stuff it into a smallish body with the kinds of items that the baby boomers wanted, such as bucket seats, Hurst shifters, and "mag"-style wheels? True, some factory Super Stocks, particularly the Mopars, had big engines in light bodies, but they were built for the hardcore racer and were more at home at the drag strip than on the highway.

DeLorean's GTO changed all that. This Pontiac was a fully equipped, practical street machine. It was not powered by a temperamental, detuned race engine. Thanks to a special hydraulic camshaft, a moderate compression ratio, and dual exhausts, it was a fairly mild automobile—until

New package
of instant action:
Olds ⟨4 4 2⟩

What's the 4-4-2? Just the sweetest piece of live action on wheels! Small wonder, too, when you check its credentials. An all-new, all-its-own 400-cubic-inch V-8. Four-barrel carb. Twin pipes. Heavy-duty suspension. Nylon red-line tires. Three smooth transmission availabilities: 3-speed synchromesh, close-ratio 4-on-the-floor or Jetaway automatic. You can tuck all this "instant action" into any F-85 V-8 coupe or convertible. And 4-4-2 prices start below any other high-performance car in America designed for every-day driving. Sound like your kind of action? See your Oldsmobile Dealer. He has your number: 4-4-2! Oldsmobile Division • General Motors Corp.

'65 ⟨ OLDSMOBILE
The Rocket Action Car!

In the mid-sixties, the normally reserved Oldsmobile corporation was hankering for a bigger slice of the youthful GTO market. For 1965 it dropped its new 400-cubic-inch V8 into the 4-4-2.

you hit the gas pedal. Then, watch out—especially if you opted for 3x2 carburetion.

What the GTO had going for it more than anything was image. Backed by an aggressive advertising campaign (the brainchild of ad executive–drag racer Jim Wangers), it achieved legend status overnight. Who could resist the call?

For the man who wouldn't mind riding a tiger if someone'd only put wheels on it...

The GTO was as coveted by American teenagers as a date with a homecoming queen. And why not? The GTO had unadulterated sex appeal and promised unheard-of thrills. From its Italian name (Gran Turismo Omologato, stolen right from Ferrari) to its scooped hood and Hurst floor shifter, the Goat had it all.

Wangers engineered a media blitz. There was GTO cologne for men, the "GeeTo Tiger" 45 rpm record, and GTO driving shoes from Thom McAn. Severely tweaked test cars ensured that all magazine reports would include startling acceleration figures. Though Wangers denies it today, it has long been rumored that the test cars were often equipped with 421 engines, not 389s. In a 1993 interview with journalist Michael Breeding, Jack "Doc" Watson, who worked for Hurst Performance back then, said he knows that they had 421s "because I put 'em there." The truth probably lies somewhere in the middle.

Pontiac made sure everyone knew you had a GTO, too. Six GTO emblems adorned each car's sparkling flanks, and in case you forgot what you were driving once you were inside, there was another posted on the dashboard.

The exhaust was specially tuned for just the right sound, although nothing could match the song of the three 2-barrel carbs at full throttle on a warm summer night. It was music for young America.

One of the more amusing aspects of the GTO's success is that by corporate edict an engine that large couldn't be installed in a car of that size. DeLorean snuck it past the suits on GM's fourteenth floor as an option on the Tempest. The same executives went ballistic until they realized that the plant couldn't process the orders fast enough.

The heart and soul of any muscle car is its engine, and the GTO was no exception. Pontiac took a standard 10.75:1 compression Bonneville 389, added 421 H.O. cylinder heads, a split-duration hydraulic cam, and either 4-barrel (325 hp) or 6-barrel (348 hp) induction. The 3-speed manual was standard; options for the automatic included a 4-speed and beefed-up 2-speed.

Wanna talk about bargain prices? In its first year, the GTO was actually a $295.90 option on the popular LeMans, which had base prices of $2,491 (coupe), $2,556 (hardtop), and $2,796 (convertible). When the sales figures were added up, a total of 32,450 GTOs—more than six times the initial allotment—had moved out the door.

America had a new hero on its hands.

My Rocket 88

The success of the Pontiac with the funny foreign name floored the rest of the industry. The first retaliatory strike was launched by Pontiac's sister division Oldsmobile, which had previously stayed out of the supercar war. Oldsmobile's F-85 had the same basic chassis as the GTO, and it was only natural that a hotted-up Rocket V8 would be readied to compete.

Thus, Olds introduced the 4-4-2 option package. The name stood for its 4-barrel carburetor, 4-speed transmission, and dual exhausts. To get one, you ordered R.P.O. B09, the Police Apprehender package. This gave you high-compression pistons, a high-lift cam, and a twin-snorkel air cleaner. These goodies, which were bolted to the 330 V8, made for a fairly decent package. Plus, the engineers threw in a very capable heavy-duty suspension, which included heavy-duty springs and a then unheard-of rear stabilizer bar. (Because the four-door model was an option on the F-85, it was possible to get a four-door 4-4-2. Seven of these cars were built in 1964.)

While the 4-4-2's 310 horsepower put it at a serious disadvantage compared to the competition, its driveability offered plenty of consolation. What this car really needed was an injection of excitement—compared to the GTO, it was fairly tame.

The success of the Pontiac intermediate really stung Chevrolet, which fancied itself as having a lock on the youth market. True, it had the Chevelle SS, but the base engine for that car was an in-line

PONTIAC

1964

Cu. In.	389	
Bore (in.)	4.06	
Stroke (in.)	3.75	
Compression	10.75:1	
Induction	1x4 bbl.	3x2 bbl.
Horsepower/RPM	325/4800	348/4800
Torque (lbs.-ft.)/RPM	428/3200	428/3600

1964 (cont.)

Cu. In.	421		
Bore (in.)	4.09		
Stroke (in.)	4.00		
Compression	10.50:1	10.75:1	
Induction	1x4 bbl.	3x2 bbl.	
Horsepower/RPM	320/4400	350/4600	370/5200
Torque (lbs.-ft.)/RPM	455/2800	454/3200	460/3800

1965

Cu. In.	389		421
Bore (in.)	4.06		4.09
Stroke (in.)	3.75		4.00
Compression	10.75:1		10.75:1
Induction	1x4 bbl.	3x2 bbl.	3x2 bbl.
Horsepower/RPM	335/5000	360/5200	376/5000
Torque (lbs.-ft.)/RPM	431/3200	424/3600	461/3600

1966

Cu. In.	389		421
Bore (in.)	4.06		4.09
Stroke (in.)	3.75		4.00
Compression	10.75:1		10.75:1
Induction	1x4 bbl.	3x2 bbl.	3x2 bbl.
Horsepower/RPM	335/5000	360/5200	376/5000
Torque (lbs.-ft.)/RPM	431/3200	424/3600	461/3600

1967

Cu. In.	400		
Bore (in.)	4.12		
Stroke (in.)	3.75		
Compression	10.75:1		
Induction	1x4 bbl.		
Horsepower/RPM	335/5000	360/5100	360/5400
Torque (lbs.-ft.)/RPM	441/3400	438/3600	438/3800

Buoyed by the success of the GTO, Oldsmobile created the 4-4-2 using parts from the police bins. The name originally referred to a 4-barrel carb, 4-speed trans, and dual exhausts, but by 1965 4-4-2 meant a standard 400-cubic-inch engine.

Dr. Oldsmobile Goes Racing

During a two-week period in June 1966, Oldsmobile built fifty-four W-30 Force-Air Induction 6-barrel cars. This was done in order to legalize the cars for NHRA drag racing, whose rules required that fifty be built. The vehicles came down a regular assembly line and each ram air cleaner was stamped with a number, though the numbers were not necessarily put on cars in the order they were built. For example, it is known that car No. 4 was produced after later-numbered cars.

The three 2-barrel carbs were fed fresh air by 5-inch flexible fabric hoses that were reinforced with wire and ran from the chrome air cleaner to 7¾-inch x 3½-inch ducts located in the front bumper at the parking light location. This required changes to the bumper and meant the parking lamps had to be relocated. A radical 308-degree, 0.474-inch-lift hydraulic cam offered a flatter power curve and improved valve springs; 1.6:1 rocker arms were part of the package, too. Valve size was 2.06 inches on the intake side and 1.629 on the exhaust. A different oil pump spring increased pressure.

Higher-capacity axles were used in the rear and all fifty-four vehicles came with 4.11 gears. The final change for racing consisted of relocating the battery to the trunk for better weight transfer. Price was $279 for the W-30 package, a bargain even in 1960s dollars.

According to Mike Furman, an Oldsmobile enthusiast who owns car No. 4 and has much of the original factory paperwork on the W-30s, many of these were painted outlandish colors to make them stand out at the track. Among the weird color combinations were gold with a black roof and a red interior, and Tasco turquoise with a yellow roof and a turquoise interior. The fifty-four W-30 Oldsmobiles broke down as follows: twenty-five F-85 Holiday coupes, eight F-85 Sport coupes, sixteen Cutlass hardtops, and five Cutlass Sport coupes.

Of those fifty-four, ten were shipped to Holiday Oldsmobile in Minneapolis. One of these was destroyed in a fatal car crash involving the son of Holiday's owner. Only twelve are known to exist today; three of those are radio/heater delete cars. None had air-conditioning and only one had power steering and brakes.

Their value today is in the $50,000 range, but let the buyer beware: the Force-Air Induction hardware was also sold over the counter as the Track Pack and many enthusiasts built their own.

While most of the 54 W-30 Force-Air Induction 6-barrel cars built by Oldsmobile were cut-rate sedans with oddball paint schemes, this one was built using a hardtop body and was painted a subtle Autumn Bronze metallic paint.

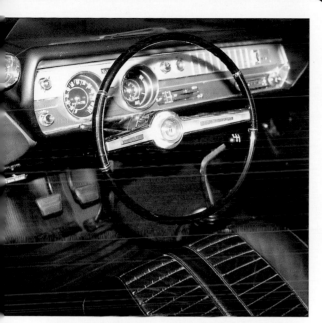

In the 1966 W-30 Oldsmobiles, fresh air was fed from ducts located in the bumper to a trio of two-barrel carbs. The cleaners were numbered 1 to 54 to correspond to the number of the vehicle in which they were installed. Options included the factory tachometer located in the upper left corner of the dash (above), but not air-conditioning.

6-cylinder. The Corvette's 300-horse 327, which was available as an option, moved fairly well, but it nonetheless left the Bowtie Brigade sucking GTO exhaust fumes for a long time. The 409 was optional in the restyled, full-size '64 Chevys, but those boxy cars had little in the way of sex appeal.

Ford had problems similar to Chevrolet's. Although one could get a 271-horsepower 289 in the midsize Fairlane, this wasn't enough—the 289 couldn't compete with a big block. The 427 Galaxies were movers, but they were very heavy. And by the end of 1964, Ford was busy trying to keep up with orders for its new Mustang, which provoked a frenzy among car buyers of all ages.

Going To Drag City

Over at Chrysler, the midsize cars were being freshened up for the third year in a row and the designers finally came up with pleasing cues that were attractive—still undeniably Mopar, but pretty nonetheless. Thanks to this redesign and plenty of screaming engines, sales rose almost 20 percent

OLDSMOBILE

1964

Cu. In.	330
Bore (in.)	3.94
Stroke (in.)	3.39
Compression	10.25:1
Induction	1x4 bbl.
Horsepower/RPM	310/5200
Torque (lbs.-ft.)/RPM	355/3600

1965

Cu. In.	400
Bore (in.)	4.00
Stroke (in.)	3.975
Compression	10.25:1
Induction	1x4 bbl.
Horsepower/RPM	345/4800
Torque (lbs.-ft.)/RPM	440/3200

1966

Cu. In.	400	
Bore (in.)	4.00	
Stroke (in.)	3.975	
Compression	10.50:1	
Induction	1x4 bbl.	3x2 bbl.
Horsepower/RPM	350/5000	360/5000
Torque (lbs.-ft.)/RPM	440/3600	440/3600

1967

Cu. In.	400
Bore (in.)	4.00
Stroke (in.)	3.975
Compression	10.50:1
Induction	1x4 bbl.
Horsepower/RPM	350/5000
Torque (lbs.-ft.)/RPM	440/3600

over 1963. The hot new street mill was the 426-S (which stood for Street). Most people called it the Street Wedge. It was not a detuned version of the fabulous Max Wedge, but basically a long-stroke 383 passenger-car engine rated at 365 horses at 4800 rpm.

While the 426-S was competitive with the GTO and far ahead of the other muscle cars, it didn't have the unbridled performance of the Max Wedges. It was, however, far more "streetable." The year 1964 was also notable in that it marked Chrysler's introduction of the near-bulletproof A-833 4-speed, just what its muscle cars needed.

In 1964 Chrysler also released the Stage III version of the Max Wedge. This was the deadliest Max Wedge yet, thanks to a radical new cam, stiffer valve springs, 11:1 and 12.5:1 compression, and extensive cylinder head refinements. Still rated at 415 and 425 horsepower, these bad boys were definitely more at home in sanctioned competition than on the street.

That didn't stop the company from running such beautiful ads as the one featuring the infamous Dave Strickler's '64 Dodge Ramcharger, which took Top Stock Eliminator honors at an AHRA (American Hot Rod Association) event in Phoenix: "Dragstrip competition, stock car races, and road rallies continue to confirm Chrysler Corporation Engineering...Want to eliminate all other cars? Test drive a '64 from Chrysler Corporation." Or "Meet the 'Orange Monster'—Plymouth's explosive Super Stock 426-III." It was poetry for gearheads back then.

By far, the most important news of 1964 if you were a Mopar maniac was the return of the Hemi. For that year Chrysler produced its first hemispherical head engine since the fifties, and it was available as a race-only piece. You could get the Hemi in a lightweight or steel-bodied drag car or in a steel-bodied NASCAR stocker. Fifty-five race Hemis were built for both Plymouth and Dodge in 1964, but this engine's heyday as a street terror was still two years away.

Who's afraid of Plymouth's "Orange Monster"?

Every other super stock on the strip—that's who!

Above left: The cast-iron Max Wedge exhaust manifolds were awfully heavy, but today they are worth their weight in gold. **Above right:** By 1964 the Plymouth Sport Fury (top) and its Dodge cousins had evolved into beautifully styled automobiles. Bucket seats, consoles, and the new A-833 4-speed made cars like this 426 Street Wedge wonderful street-strip machines. By 1964 development of the Chrysler Max Wedge engine (bottom) had reached an all-time high. This engine was brutal on the competition, but the introduction of the 426 race Hemi made it superfluous.

Stylists greatly enhanced the looks of the '64 Sport Fury by completely redesigning the front fascia. Gone were the unusually spaced quad headlights and jutting grille of the previous two model years. The result was a 20 percent increase in sales that year.

The 1965 GTO was updated with a single hood scoop that could be made functional, stacked headlights, and a full-width taillight treatment. With the optional dealer-installed Ram Air kits, these cars really ran.

BUICK

1965

Cu. In.	401	425*
Bore (in.)	4.19	4.31
Stroke (in.)	3.64	3.64
Compression	10.25:1	10.25:1
Induction	1x4 bbl.	2x4 bbl.
Horsepower/RPM	325/4400	360/4400
Torque (lbs.-ft.)/RPM	445/2800	465/2800

* Optional Riviera GS only

1966

Cu. In.	401
Bore (in.)	4.19
Stroke (in.)	3.64
Compression	10.25:1
Induction	1x4 bbl.
Horsepower/RPM	325/4400
Torque (lbs.-ft.)/RPM	445/2800

1967

Cu. In.	340	400
Bore (in.)	3.75	4.04
Stroke (in.)	3.85	3.90
Compression	10.25:1	10.25:1
Induction	1x4 bbl.	1x4 bbl.
Horsepower/RPM	260/4200	340/5000
Torque (lbs.-ft.)/RPM	365/2800	440/3200

Competition Improves the Breed

Pontiac capitalized on the success of the GTO by freshening up its looks with stacked headlights, a new scooped hood, and wraparound taillights. The frame was beefed up, and horsepower was up to 335 in 4V trim and 360 with three deuces, thanks to new cams. By midyear, a Ram Air kit was offered as a dealer-installed option. This option consisted of a sheet-metal tub that went around the tops of the three carbs under the air cleaner and was sealed to the underside of the hood with a thick foam-rubber gasket. All you had to do was remove the metal plugs in the scoop. It was worth about 10 horsepower and added further to the GTO legend. Sales skyrocketed, with 75,352 '65s flooding the streets by the end of the year.

Working off the GTO's image, Pontiac played up the 2+2, a Catalina hardtop–based "gentleman's GTO" that had been introduced in 1964. The standard engine was a 325-horse 389, but it could be stuffed full of 421 H.O. with 376 hp and a 4-speed transmission. As if to show he wasn't above fiddling with full-size test cars either,

Wangers slipped *Car and Driver* a Royal Pontiac–prepped 2+2 that was reported to have run 0 to 60 mph in a physics-defying 3.9 seconds.

With all of these developments, these were truly great days to be an automobile enthusiast.

Even conservative Buick—purveyor of doctors' cars—finally joined the party. By taking the 401-cube V8 out of its Wildcat and slipping it into the unsuspecting Skylark, Buick engineers created the Gran Sport. The ads called it "A Howitzer With Windshield Wipers."

The engine itself was dubbed the "Wildcat 445"; the number represented its peak torque rating (at 2800 rpm). Horsepower was 325 at 4800 rpm and transmission choices were the standard 3-speed manual, the optional 4-speed stick, or a 2-speed automatic with Buick's innovative "switch pitch" torque converter.

To ensure that the vehicle was up to the rigors of high horsepower, all Gran Sports were built on the convertible's heavy-duty boxed frame. For improved handling, a fatter anti-roll bar was employed up front, while a 4–control arm suspension was used out back to help control side-to-side movement and axle hop.

Inside were standard bucket seats and a floor shift. The tachometer was optional, as was air-conditioning. In keeping with the less-than-safety-conscious attitude prevalent in mid-sixties America, the seat belts could be deleted for credit.

"Ever prodded a throttle with 445 lb.-ft. of torque coiled tightly at the end of it?" asked one Gran Sport print advertisement. "Do that with one of these and you can start billing yourself as The Human Cannonball."

Not long after the 4-4-2 was introduced in 1964, Oldsmobile started making plans to fit a new 400-cubic-inch V8 into it. The Rocket V8 for 1965 had a raised deck height, beefier bottom end, dual exhaust, and 345 horsepower. Now it was nipping at the heels of the big dogs. Also, 1965 was the first year you could order an automatic transmission in the 4-4-2.

While waiting for its new 396 big block to arrive in the spring of 1965, Chevrolet made the

A Howitzer with windshield wipers? That's what Buick claimed its new '65½ Skylark Gran Sport (above) was, thanks to the 401 engine transplant from its Wildcat big brother (top left).
The '65 Chevelle (top right) was pleasing to look at, but its 350-horsepower 327 engine was no match for Tri-Power GTO.

The '67 Dodge R/T (above) and its Plymouth GTX stablemate constituted Chrysler's first attempts to create a "GTO-style" muscle car. Thanks to its 440-cubic-inch engine (and optional 426 Hemi), the R/T could shake almost anything on the road.

DODGE/PLYMOUTH

1964

Cu. In.	383	426-S
Bore (in.)	4.25	4.25
Stroke (in.)	3.38	3.75
Compression	10.00:1	10.30:1
Induction	1x4 bbl.	1x4 bbl.
Horsepower/RPM	330/4600	365/4800
Torque (lbs.-ft.)/RPM	425/2800	470/3200

1964 (cont.)

Cu. In.	426		
Bore (in.)	4.25		
Stroke (in.)	3.75		
Compression	11.00:1	12.50:1	12.50:1*
Induction	2x4 bbl.	2x4 bbl.	2x4 bbl.
Horsepower/RPM	415/5600	425/5600	425/6000
Torque (lbs.-ft.)/RPM	470/4400	480/4400	480/4600

*Race Hemi

1965

Cu. In.	273	383	426-S
Bore (in.)	3.63	4.25	4.25
Stroke (in.)	3.31	3.38	3.75
Compression	10.50:1	10.00:1	10.30:1
Induction	1x4 bbl.	1x4 bbl.	1x4 bbl.
Horsepower/RPM	235/5200	330/4600	365/4800
Torque (lbs.-ft.)/RPM	280/4000	425/2800	470/3200

1965 (cont.)

Cu. In.	426
Bore (in.)	4.25
Stroke (in.)	3.75
Compression	12.50:1*
Induction	2x4 bbl.
Horsepower/RPM	425/6000
Torque (lbs.-ft.)/RPM	480/4600

*Race Hemi

1966

Cu. In.	273	383
Bore (in.)	3.63	4.25
Stroke (in.)	3.31	3.38
Compression	10.50:1	10.00:1
Induction	1x4 bbl.	1x4 bbl.
Horsepower/RPM	235/5200	325/4800
Torque (lbs.-ft.)/RPM	280/4000	425/2800

1966 (cont.)

Cu. In.	426*
Bore (in.)	4.25
Stroke (in.)	3.75
Compression	10.25:1
Induction	2x4 bbl.
Horsepower/RPM	425/5000
Torque (lbs.-ft.)/RPM	490/4000

*Street Hemi

1967

Cu. In.	273	383
Bore (in.)	3.63	4.25
Stroke (in.)	3.31	3.38
Compression	10.50:1	10.00:1
Induction	1x4 bbl.	1x4 bbl.
Horsepower/RPM	235/5200	325/4800
Torque (lbs.-ft.)/RPM	280/4000	425/2800

1967 (cont.)

Cu. In.	426*	440
Bore (in.)	4.25	4.32
Stroke (in.)	3.75	3.75
Compression	10.25:1	10.00:1
Induction	2x4 bbl.	1x4 bbl.
Horsepower/RPM	425/5000	375/4600
Torque (lbs.-ft.)/RPM	490/4000	480/3200

*Street Hemi

Corvette's 350-horse 327 available in the Chevelle. This car was a real mover, especially since you could get it in a totally stripped-down model. But it was the 396 with its splayed valve arrangement that made people swoon.

Chevy teased the anxiously awaiting automobile world by building only 201 examples of the RPO Z-16 for 1965. Packing the punch for this was a 375-horsepower version of the 396 (full-size Chevys had versions with 325 and 425 horsepower), with a hot hydraulic lifter cam, 11:1 compression, big-valve rectangular port heads, a giant Holley 4-barrel carburetor, and an aluminum intake manifold. It made 420 lbs.-ft. of torque at 3600 rpm.

Like its big-bore cousins from GM's other divisions, the Z-16 was more than just a huge engine in a standard intermediate body. The Chevelle had an upgraded suspension with front and rear roll bars, quicker steering, and a larger rear axle. All had the M21 Muncie 4-speed transmission.

Outside, the Z-16 had a unique tail, revised emblems, and simulated 5-spoke "mag" wheel covers. The interior was highlighted by a 160 mph speedometer and six-grand tach.

Z-16s went for almost $4,500 each (about $1,000 more than a '65 GTO), and are worth a small fortune today. They could bully anything GM sold except a fuel-injected or 396/425-horse Sting Ray.

The Corvette got its own version of the 396, with a solid lifter camshaft, special exhaust manifolds, and other goodies. Its low price (a $292.70 option) spelled doom for the more sophisticated, less powerful 375-hp 327 "fuelie" engine.

Dodge and Plymouth offered fresh styling and an engine lineup that was basically a carryover from 1964. Gone were the push-button automatic transmissions, thanks to a government mandate that standardized the industry. The 330-horsepower 383 and 365-horse 426 were the motors of choice for enthusiasts. Ads aimed at them bragged about the Coronet being the "Animal Tamer."

Chrysler also concentrated on its racing successes in its advertising. "Our new 426 Coronet ought to have its head examined. You know what the Hemi is...It's got valves as big as stove lids. A plug jammed right in the middle of the combustion chamber. 426 cubes...Why not drop a Hemi in the new Coronet 500?"

Ford got a break in 1965 when NASCAR and USAC (United States Auto Club) banned Chrysler's Hemi from super speedway competition. With that beast banished, the contingent from Dearborn ruled NASCAR with an iron fist. It ended up with forty-eight victories for the season. Defend-ing champion Richard Petty ended up drag racing a '65 Hemi-powered Barracuda dubbed "43 Jr." Painted Petty Blue, it had the word "Outlawed" splashed across the side and it sported a Plymouth bumper sticker out back that chided NASCAR: "If you can't outrun 'em, outlaw 'em."

The year 1965 was a monumental one for Chevrolet's Corvette (above). Production of the legendary fuel-injected small block (top right), now making 375 horsepower, ended midway through the year; the small block was replaced by the fire-breathing 425-horse 396.

The '66 Dodge Charger (top) was only marginally successful in the marketplace. Its standard hideaway headlights, four bucket seats, and optional Hemi power make it a collectible today, while its quirky styling makes it a favorite among... well, quirky people. The Charger was derived from the '66–'67 Coronet body (above).

Beauty and the Beast

That's what you got when you put the awesome new-for-1966 Street Hemi in Dodge's latest image maker, the Charger. The Charger name was no stranger to Pentastar fans. It was culled from one of the factory-backed supercharged A/FX machines, and there were two radical show cars that shared its moniker. But for Mopar enthusiasts who had waited for something really distinctive, the Charger was a futuristic, turntable show vehicle available at your local Dodge dealer. Best of all, it was available with a throbbing Street Hemi engine.

Cynics will say that the Charger was nothing more than a Coronet with some fancy hideaway headlights, a fastback roof grafted on, and a tricked-out interior. But the Charger was much more than this—it was the perfect showcase for the 426 Street Hemi. Chrysler had gone to great lengths in its advertising to tout the Hemi's mighty record on the race tracks since it was reintroduced in 1964. To reverse its image on the street and grab a piece of the GTO market, the folks from Highland Park needed something with real pizzazz. The Charger's

CHEVROLET

1964			
Cu. In.	409		
Bore (In.)	4.31		
Stroke (in.)	3.50		
Compression	10.00:1	11.00:1	
Induction	1x4 bbl.	1x4 bbl.	2x4 bbl.
Horsepower/RPM	340/5000	400/5800	425/6000
Torque (lbs.-ft.)/RPM	420/3200	425/3600	425/4200

1965	
Cu. In.	327
Bore (in.)	4.00
Stroke (in.)	3.25
Compression	11.00:1
Induction	1x4 bbl.
Horsepower/RPM	350/5800
Torque (lbs.-ft.)/RPM	360/3600

1965 (cont.)		
Cu. In.	396	
Bore (in.)	4.094	
Stroke (in.)	3.76	
Compression	10.25:1	11.00:1
Induction	1x4 bbl.	1x4 bbl.
Horsepower/RPM	325/4800	425/6400
Torque (lbs.-ft.)/RPM	410/3200	415/4000

1965 (cont.)		
Cu. In.	409	
Bore (in.)	4.31	
Stroke (in.)	3.50	
Compression	10.00:1	11.00:1
Induction	1x4 bbl.	1x4 bbl.
Horsepower/RPM	340/5000	400/5800
Torque (lbs.-ft.)/RPM	420/3200	425/3600

1966	
Cu. In.	327
Bore (in.)	4.00
Stroke (in.)	3.25
Compression	11.00:1
Induction	1x4 bbl.
Horsepower/RPM	350/5800
Torque (lbs.-ft.)/RPM	360/3600

1966 (cont.)			
Cu. In.	396		
Bore (in.)	4.094		
Stroke (in.)	3.76		
Compression	10.25:1		11.00:1
Induction	1x4 bbl.		1x4 bbl.
Horsepower/RPM	325/4800	360/5200	375/5600
Torque (lbs.-ft.)/RPM	410/3200	420/3600	415/3600

1966 (cont.)		
Cu. In.	427	
Bore (in.)	4.25	
Stroke (in.)	3.76	
Compression	10.25:1	11.00:1
Induction	1x4 bbl.	1x4 bbl.
Horsepower/RPM	390/5200	425/5600
Torque (lbs.-ft.)/RPM	470/3600	460/4400

1967	
Cu. In.	327
Bore (in.)	4.00
Stroke (in.)	3.25
Compression	11.00:1
Induction	1x4 bbl.
Horsepower/RPM	350/5800
Torque (lbs.-ft.)/RPM	360/3600

1967 (cont.)			
Cu. In.	396		
Bore (in.)	4.094		
Stroke (in.)	3.76		
Compression	10.25:1		11.00:1
Induction	1x4 bbl.		1x4 bbl.
Horsepower/RPM	325/4800	350/5200	375/5600
Torque (lbs.-ft.)/RPM	410/3200	415/3400	415/3600

1967 (cont.)			
Cu. In.	427		
Bore (in.)	4.25		
Stroke (in.)	3.76		
Compression	10.25:1		11.00:1
Induction	1x4 bbl.	3x2 bbl.	3x2 bbl.
Horsepower/RPM	390/5400	400/5400	435/5800
Torque (lbs.-ft.)/RPM	460/3600	460/3600	460/4000

The Chevelle (above) finally became a contender in the muscle car wars with the introduction of the 396 engine option (right) late in 1965. The limited production of this version of the Chevelle kept it out of the hands of the general public, but this car is highly prized by collectors today.

motorized hideaway headlights (still something of a rarity back then) were rotated into position and the area around the lights had the same pattern as the grille itself, so when the lights were in use the grille still looked uniform—it was as if the lights appeared by magic. Truthfully, magic was something Charger owners often needed, given the system's propensity for breaking down.

The rest of the Charger's styling was equally unusual. The big, sloping roof made it a natural for NASCAR's speedways, as well as for getting attention at the local cruise spots. Inside were front and rear bucket seats, which could be divided by an optional full-length console, and gauges that sprouted from the instrument panel and seemed to glow from behind with fluorescent light. And while Dodge's smaller 318 and 361 engines were available, and a 325 hp 383 was there for enthusiasts on a budget, those who desired nothing less than all-out performance could opt for the Street Hemi.

To get the Hemi homologated for NASCAR, Chrysler had to make it a regular production option. For streetability, it was fitted with a pair of Carter 4-barrel carbs, 10.25:1 compression, cast-iron heads with softer springs, and a less radical solid-lifter camshaft. And that's about it. Purchasing an automobile with a Street Hemi was as close as you could come to buying a NASCAR stocker for highway use.

For $907.60, you got the Hemi with a heavy-duty suspension and brakes and Goodyear Blue Streak nylon tires. But you also had to take the heavy-duty TorqueFlite automatic ($206.30) or 4-speed manual transmission ($184.20) as a mandatory option. In return, you got mind-bending performance and instant celebrity status at the burger stand.

Today, the Street Hemis rank among the most sought-after automobiles in the world. Who can argue with 425 horsepower at 5000 rpm or 490 lbs.-ft. of torque at 4000? Even wrapped in plain Belvedere sheet metal (it was available in the Satellite and Coronet, too), the cars were feared.

Car and Driver got one to go 0 to 60 in just 5.3 seconds and cover the quarter-mile in 13.8 seconds at 104 mph. This is startling performance today; forget that this car weighed over 4,000 pounds with driver and test equipment and that it was running on standard bias-ply tires, which were incapable of harnessing that kind of horsepower and torque. Given a set of drag slicks, you could cut one second off the quarter-mile ET.

A Star Is Born

Thanks to the excitement surrounding the Z-16 Chevelles of 1965, there was plenty of momentum to carry buyers into the showrooms to check out the '66 SS396 Chevelles. All-new styling gave the car a substantially tougher appearance.

Standard in the SS396 was a 325-horse version of the big-block Chevy. Next up was a 360-horsepower version with a 4-bolt main block, a larger carb, and a bumpier camshaft. For all-out street thrashing, there was the 396/375 L78, which was almost identical to the engine rated at 425 horsepower in the Corvette the year before. Although it lacked the 'Vette's free-flowing exhaust manifolds, the SS396 did have the 'Vette's rather aggressive solid-lifter cam, rectangular port heads, and Holley carb on an aluminum intake. Over the

The '66 Chevelle grew in size and sales were helped by the widespread availability of the 396 engine, which could be had with up to 375 horsepower. This made the Chevelle a real challenger to the GTO.

With classic lines like these, it's no wonder the '66 GTO was the bestselling muscle car of all time. Buoyed by its new "venturi" styling and under-the-hood improvements in the carburetion and camshaft departments, the Wide-Track division moved 96,946 Tigers in 1966.

years, the SS396 would prove to be second in popularity only to the GTO.

If you wanted a real sleeper, Chevrolet had just the ticket. In 1966 they stuffed the L79 350-horsepower Corvette 327 into the diminutive Chevy II SS. The 327 had big valves, a high-lift hydraulic cam, and 11:1 compression. This much engine in a compact car gave the previously unrespected Nova real eye-opening performance. They had no trouble running with muscle cars that offered 100 more cubic inches. In fact, Bill "Grumpy" Jenkins, behind the wheel of a Chevy II SS, gave even the Hemicars fits in NHRA A/Stock. The L79 Chevy II had barely caught on when Chevy mysteriously pulled the plug on it just six cars into the 1967 model year. For 1966, 5,481 of these pocket rockets found their way into buyers' hands.

Buoyed by the GTO's success in the marketplace, Pontiac made that car a specific model in 1966. No longer would it just be an option on a lesser vehicle. Customers responded to this newfound freedom by buying 96,946 units, an all-time high for any muscle car.

The GTO's new "venturi" styling, with a revised grille and louvered taillights, was breathtaking. It had an updated cockpit and and an improved engine. While the standard 4-barrel mill was a carryover, the Tri-Power option received a larger center carb, and a better cam and valve springs came with the Ram Air package. Its horsepower rating stayed the same, even if you ordered Ram Air, but you couldn't fool the public. It was a winner.

Then the brain trust at GM handed down yet another corporate edict, this one outlawing multiple

carb setups on its passenger vehicles for 1967. This was designed to squelch warranty headaches at the dealership level. (Corvettes were exempt from this because they were considered sports cars.) The multi-carb ban meant that 1966 was the last year you could order a Tri-Power Goat. This ban marked the end of an era.

But Pontiac wasn't the only GM division offering multiple carburetion in 1966. Oldsmobile, GM's "technology" division, devised a 3x2 setup for its 4-4-2. While the standard 4-barrel 400 was rated at 350 horses, the L69 "trips" upped the ante to 360 at 5,000 rpm. All told, there were 2,129 L69-equipped 4-4-2s produced, and they were real screamers but still not the top rung of the Olds performance ladder. If you wanted the most aggressive Oldsmobile, you got a '66 W-30.

1964–1967: AMERICA GETS ITS GOAT—AND A WHOLE LOT MORE

Bull's-Eye: The Big-Block Darts

In 1969 Chrysler showed how serious it was about muscle car performance by installing the 440 from its intermediate-size Dodge R/T and Plymouth GTX (left) into the compact-size Dodge Dart (above).

Among the less heralded (but no less potent) Mopars of the sixties was the 383 Dodge Dart. Shoehorning the B-motor between the frame rails on the compact A-body platform wasn't easy, but it sure was worth it. Only 457 of these machines were built in 1967. Handling was poor and braking was inadequate, but if you wanted to kick some tail at the drags, this was the car to have.

Factory horsepower was only 280 at 4200 rpm, but this was due mostly to the miserable, restrictive factory exhaust manifolds, which were contoured to clear the steering box, which lacked any sort of power assist system. In fact, the entire exhaust system was

of smaller-diameter pipes than those used on the intermediate 383s.

Production increased to 2,190 in 1968. Power was up to 300 ponies, due in large part to the new heads and cam from the Road Runner/Super Bee 383 and R/T-GTX 440. Additional power came from a new intake manifold design, a larger-diameter exhaust, and a new Carter AVS 4-barrel. There were 1,989 383 Darts built in 1969 and horsepower was up again, now to 330 at 5200.

Like your muscle cars rare? Try to find a '69 383 Dart convertible. There were thirty-nine automatics and thirty-four 4-speeds built, and very few of them survive today.

"How to Cook a Tiger"

With not-so-subtle élan, the Ford Fairlane and its Mercury Cyclone cousin finally received doses of big-block power in 1966. Both got a 335-horse version of the 390 (underrated so the cars could get into a lower drag-strip class) and the Cyclone was even chosen as the Indy Pace Car that year. Ford outfitted the 390 with a high-lift cam, a 600 cfm Holley carburetor, and dual exhausts.

Again the main competition was Pontiac's GTO, and one of the Fairlane advertisements provided a recipe for "How to Cook a Tiger," which included a listing of all the Fairlane's high-performance goodies. The photo was a close-up of a Fairlane GTA front end with a tiger tail coming out from under the hood. The GTA nomenclature stood for GT-Automatic and cars so equipped had a Ford Sport Shift that could be shifted like a regular automatic or manually, with detents that prevented you from missing a gear.

While the 390 was a willing performer, those with the bucks could opt for a full-boogie version of the 427 medium riser, which made 425 horsepower, or a 410-horse single 4-barrel, which was also available. Both were nothing short of race cars in plain-Jane disguise, with fiberglass hoods, modified shock towers, and a total lack of sound deadeners and undercoating. Only fifty-seven were ever built, again to quality them for the NHRA's Super Stock ranks.

When the Beach Boys' "Good Vibrations" started blasting through car radios in October 1966, the new '67 models were just rolling into showrooms around the country. It was the perfect theme song for the year—cruisin' Main Street was never better. What vibes could be finer than those from a 6000 rpm power-shift in a 400-plus hp muscle car?

Chrysler finally got on the supercar scoreboard in 1967 with the introduction of its Plymouth GTX and Dodge R/T. Based on the Belvedere and Coronet, respectively, the "letter" cars had all the

go of their predecessors and then some, but they also had plenty of GTO-style panache and flair.

What really set them apart was the standard engine: 440 cubic inches of ground-pounding excitement. Making 375 horsepower and 480 lbs.-ft. of torque, the 440 was the largest engine yet installed in a muscle car.

Both were outstanding, visually. The GTX had dual hood scoops (nonfunctional), a flip-open gas cap on the left rear fender, a revised trim panel in the decklid, and an updated grille with quad headlights. Twin stripes running the length of the hood and trunk were optional. The R/T had ultraclean styling with a unique grille, faux louvers on the hood, and the taillights integrated into a matching trunk filler panel.

The 440s sprang from the 413-426 RB engine family and actually had appeared in mild tune in Chrysler's bigger cars a year earlier. In Dodge Magnum and Plymouth Super Commando trim, they sported special big-port heads, a strong hydraulic cam, beefed-up bottom ends, and

While it wasn't wildly popular from a sales perspective, the '67 Mercury Cyclone was an impressive performer with the expensive 427 engine option. "Dyno" Don Nicholson's '66 Eliminator I Cyclone was the first full flip-top bodied Funny Car. It was also the first Funny Car to run in the 7-second zone.

free-flowing exhaust manifolds with an H-pipe between the twice pipes for more bottom-end power.

Four-speed cars came equipped with the sturdier Dana rear and 3.54 Sure-Grip gears. TorqueFlite-equipped cars got the 8¾ rear with 3.23 gears; the Sure-Grip differential was optional. The extra cubic inches not only meant more horsepower, but also unreal torque (480 lbs.-ft.). Of course, it goes without saying that if you needed to go a little faster, you could order either the GTX or the R/T with a Street Hemi.

Car and Driver, which had had a big hand in starting GTO mania back in 1964, stoked the fires once more in its GTX road test: "Pontiac GTO lovers better take their performance image and head for the hills. The Plymouth boys have breathed new life into the old 440 engine to produce a new monster capable of blowing off everything including a Street Hemi to 100 mph."

Ford on the Floor

In 1967 Ford started pushing its 427 Fairlanes heavily in advertising, though it was mentioned that these cars weren't recommended for "highway or general passenger use." Fat chance! The fiberglass hood was gone, but you still got a tach, heavy-duty suspension, Wide Oval tires, bucket seats, and racing stripes. If you ordered a 390, you got less horsepower than the year before, thanks to a switch from a 600 cfm Holley 4-barrel to a smaller Autolite.

Back before political correctness was a concern for advertisers, Mercury billed its '67 Cyclone as "The Man's Car! For men who like their action big...options include fade resistant power disc brakes and His-and-Her Select-Shift Merc-O-Matic (lets a man run it through the gears, lets his wife leave it in automatic)."

Ford actually had quite a year with its motorsports program. Mario Andretti won the Daytona 500 in a 427 Fairlane. A.J. Foyt won his third Indy 500 in a Ford-powered Coyote and he shared the driving duties with Parnelli Jones as they pushed the Ford GT40 to victory at the 24 Hours of LeMans.

In 1967 all of GM's muscle cars got a shot in the arm, thanks to the introduction of the Turbo 400 transmission, and an added measure of safety with available disc brakes.

Pontiac made the adjustment to life without Tri-Power quite nicely, thanks to its new 400-cubic-inch V8, which was basically a bored version of the 389 with brand-new heads, a new intake, and a Rochester Quadrajet carb that flowed more air than the Carter 4-barrel it replaced. Standard in the GTO was 335 horsepower and 441 lbs.-ft. of torque, still wrapped in that mesmerizing body. Turbo 400 cars came standard with the Hurst "His-Hers" shifter, which was an honest dual-gate shifter allowing full manual or automatic shifting.

Ram Air became a factory option and the ads screamed that it came with a high-output cam (301/313 duration) and standard 4.33 gears with Saf-T-Track. Of course, the Ram Air GTO was still advertised at "just" 360 hp. This didn't stop *Car Life* from getting one to turn 13.9 seconds at 104 at the drag strip. The only downside was that the 4.33 cog limited top speed to 107 mph.

You could still order the 360-horse Force-Air W-30 Oldsmobile, but without three deuces much of the magic was gone. Still, 502 W-30s were built and 1967 marked the first year these cars were equipped with red plastic inner fender liners (to reduce the vehicle's weight). In regular 4-4-2s, a 350-horse 400 was standard.

Also in 1967, Buick abandoned its fifteen-year-old nailhead V8 and brought out a more modern design, which had bigger valves and was capable of higher rpm and more horses. The top mill in the Gran Sport was the 400, which produced 340 ponies at 5000 rpm and 440 lbs.-ft. at 3200. While it made for a sweet performer, it was just a tease—an indication of some of the more ornery packages that were on the horizon.

At Chevrolet, the '67 Chevelles were carryovers mechanically from 1966—the big news was another restyle, which was only marginally successful. The optional 360-horse 396 was downgraded to 350 and the 350-horse 327 was now rated at just 325 ponies. Thankfully, the 396/375 was still around, and 411 of them were built.

The year 1967 was also the last for the fabled Sting Ray body style. Coming in 1968 was an all-new body. In fact, 1968 was a vintage year for muscle cars, as each manufacturer completely redesigned its intermediate vehicles. Between 1968 and 1970, muscle cars reached unheard-of levels of performance, style, and charisma. Unfortunately, a star always burns brightest before it burns out, and so it went with the stars of the supercar galaxy.

While most hot-foots gravitated towards the '67 Plymouth GTX, those looking for a real sleeper could order the 425-horse Hemi in the less suspicious Belvedere II Satellite body (above).

When *Car Life* magazine tested a dual quad 427 Galaxie 500 in the February 1965 issue, it ran a 14.9 at 97 mph, which indicates a severe lack of traction. "This one has more muscles than the Olympic games," they said. This example sports such sixties add-ons as the Super Stock teardrop hood and Cragar S/S wheels.

FORD

1964

Cu. In.	289
Bore (in.)	4.00
Stroke (in.)	2.87
Compression	10.50:1
Induction	1x4 bbl.
Horsepower/RPM	271/6000
Torque (lbs.-ft.)/RPM	312/3400

1964 (cont.)

Cu. In.	390	427	
Bore (in.)	4.05	4.23	
Stroke (in.)	3.78	3.78	
Compression	10.00:1	11.00:1	
Induction	1x4 bbl.	1x4 bbl.	2x4 bbl.
Horsepower/RPM	330/5000	410/5600	425/6000
Torque (lbs.-ft.)/RPM	427/3200	476/3400	480/3700

1965

Cu. In.	289
Bore (in.)	4.00
Stroke (in.)	2.87
Compression	10.50:1
Induction	1x4 bbl.
Horsepower/RPM	271/6000
Torque (lbs.-ft.)/RPM	312/3400

1965 (cont.)

Cu. In.	390	427	
Bore (in.)	4.05	4.23	
Stroke (in.)	3.78	3.78	
Compression	10.00:1	11.00:1	
Induction	1x4 bbl.	1x4 bbl.	2x4 bbl.
Horsepower/RPM	330/5000	410/5600	425/6000
Torque (lbs.-ft.)/RPM	427/3200	476/3400	480/3700

1966

Cu. In.	289	390
Bore (in.)	4.00	4.05
Stroke (in.)	2.87	3.78
Compression	10.50:1	11.00:1
Induction	1x4 bbl.	1x4 bbl.
Horsepower/RPM	271/6000	335/4800
Torque (lbs.-ft.)/RPM	312/3400	427/3200

1966 (cont.)

Cu. In.	427		428
Bore (in.)	4.23		4.13
Stroke (in.)	3.78		3.98
Compression	11.00:1		10.50:1
Induction	1x4 bbl.	2x4 bbl.	1x4 bbl.
Horsepower/RPM	410/5600	425/6000	360/5400
Torque (lbs.-ft.)/RPM	476/3400	480/3700	459/3200

1967

Cu. In.	289	390
Bore (in.)	4.00	4.05
Stroke (in.)	2.87	3.78
Compression	10.50:1	10.50:1
Induction	1x4 bbl.	1x4 bbl.
Horsepower/RPM	271/6000	320/4800
Torque (lbs.-ft.)/RPM	312/3400	427/3200

1967 (cont.)

Cu. In.	427		428
Bore (in.)	4.23		4.13
Stroke (in.)	3.78		3.98
Compression	11.00:1		10.50:1
Induction	1x4 bbl.	2x4 bbl.	1x4 bbl.
Horsepower/RPM	410/5600	425/6000	360/5400
Torque (lbs.-ft.)/RPM	476/3400	480/3700	459/3200

Ford's Thunderbolt—Heaven-Sent Performance

Although Ford didn't offer a big-engined intermediate for the street in 1964, it did take a cue from one of its high-performance dealerships and produce a number of 427-powered Fairlanes for Super Stock and A/FX competition.

The year before, Tasca Ford in East Providence, Rhode Island, had been campaigning with its homemade 427 Fairlane. Driven by Bill Lawton, this vehicle debuted at the NHRA Nationals in Indianapolis on Labor Day weekend. In this race it ran 12.21 at 118.42 (though it lost to a Z-11 Chevy). With the help of Dearborn Steel Tubing (which did the actual fabrication), Ford stuffed robust, race-prepped versions of the 427 into 1964 Fairlane bodies. The Thunderbolt was born.

Power came from a modified version of the dual-quad 427, which featured a high-rise intake manifold that required the use of a specially designed teardrop-shaped hood scoop. The manifold actually had raised intake ports, which made the height of the Holley carbs 3 inches taller than stock. Equal-length tube headers snaked through the suspension components and the carbs were fed fresh air through tubing that ran through the openings in the grille once occupied by the inboard headlamps. Thanks to internal strengthening, the 427s could turn 7000 rpm and produce over 500 horsepower.

Transmission choices were a Top Loader 4-speed with 4.44:1 gears or a beefed-up automatic with 4.58s.

Befitting a race car, all unnecessary weight was stripped from the interior, including sun visors, armrests, and sound-deadening material. The doors, hood, front fenders, and bumpers were made of fiberglass; the side windows were made of Plexiglas; and the battery was exiled to the trunk. The Thunderbolt weighed just over the 3,200-pound NHRA minimum weight. Anyone with about $3,900 could buy one at his local Ford dealer, and after all was said and done, 127 of them were built.

Although they are sometimes overshadowed by the Thunderbolts, a number of lightweight 427 Mercury Comet Cyclones were also built by the Ford Motor Company in 1964. While the majority of the Thunderbolts raced Super Stock, the Cyclones were altered to run in A/FX (so as not to compete with the Fairlanes). A total of fifty or so Cyclones were produced and they were the scourge of A/FX racing, where they ran on 10-inch tires. Most of the Thunderbolts ran in Super Stock on 7-inch tires.

The Thunderbolt Fairlanes (right) couldn't be more different from their road-going cousins. They offered nothing in the way of creature comforts and they shook at idle, thanks to the high horsepower produced by their race-prepped 427 engines (above).

The 1967 Corvette (top) is considered by many to be the finest looking and most refined of the midyear (1963–1967) 'Vettes. This one boasts big-block power and the "stinger" hood stripe. Ford's ultimate muscle car in 1966 was the 427 Fairlane (left), which had a fiberglass cold-air hood. Only 57 were ever built.

1964-1967: AMERICA GETS ITS GOAT—AND A WHOLE LOT MORE

Chapter 3

Ponycar Mania

I got a 1966 cherry red
Mustang Ford
It's got a three hundred
eighty-five horsepower
overload
You know it's way too
fast to be a-crawlin'
on these interstate
roads...

—"My Mustang Ford,"
by Chuck Berry

The '65 Mustang—introduced on April 17, 1964—was no threat on the street when equipped with the 260 V8 (above right), but it could more than hold its own when ordered with the 271-horsepower 289. Chevrolet countered Ford's ponycar with the Camaro, which offered up to 375 horsepower soon after its introduction. The '69 Z/28 (opposite) was much revered for its combination of excellent handling and its SCCA Trans-Am–inspired 302-cubic-inch V8.

If July 4 is celebrated as America's Independence Day, then perhaps it is time for Congress to declare April 17 as Independence Day for its nation's baby boomers. It was on this day in 1964 that the children of those who fought in World War II got their own special set of wheels. It was on this day that the Ford Mustang—freedom wrapped in chrome and steel—was unveiled at the New York World's Fair. More than twenty-two thousand people plunked down their cash for a Mustang the first day it was in the showrooms—buying a car would never be the same again.

Originally available as a coupe and a convertible (a fastback would come along six months later), it was a sports car with a backseat—just the right vehicle for the young and the young at heart. Demand far outstripped production, and sales for the first half-season totaled 121,538.

To give credit where credit is due, it must be stated that the Mustang was the brainchild of Lee Iacocca, the youngest general manager in Ford's history. He wanted to fill the void in the lineup created when the Thunderbird grew from a two-seat sports car to a four-seat luxury sedan. He knew there was a market for a small, sporty car; he also knew that the market for genuine two-

The top engine offered in the Mustang's first six months (all '64 Mustangs were registered as '65 models) was the solid-lifter "High Peformance 289" (above), also known as the K-motor for its option code. When stuffed in the Shelby GT350R (below), the engines were tweaked beyond 306 horsepower.

seaters was vastly limited. His idea was to make a four-passenger vehicle that was compact and sporty enough to look like a two-seater. Voilà! Instant sales sensation.

What made the Mustang even more enjoyable for Ford was that it was based on an existing platform, the inexpensive but reliable Falcon. This gave it a base price of under $2,600, and with the longest option list in the industry, a new 'Stang could be personalized for performance, luxury, or any combination thereof. Almost no one purchased a "base" Mustang.

While the Mustang couldn't be considered a pure muscle car at this point (a big-block engine wouldn't come along until 1967), it could certainly be ordered up to deliver true supercar performance. Three V8s could be ordered, right up to the solid-lifter High Performance 289 with 271 ponies. This was just the right kind of spur to put the kick in your Mustang.

When *Car and Driver* tested a '65 model with the high-winding 289 (it made its peak horsepower at 6000 rpm) and 4.11 gears, it recorded ETs of 14 seconds flat at 100 mph. This was much faster than production cars actually went; one wonders if

they were using the same driver who got a 2+2 Pontiac to go 0–60 in 3.9 seconds. Realistically, the K-motor Mustangs were high 14-, low 15-second cars.

Interestingly, a large percentage of Mustangs were being sold to women—which gave the 'Stang a reputation as a "girl's car" among hardcore enthusiasts.

Who's on First?

Though Ford caught most of the industry off guard when it released the Mustang, the competition sprang into action almost immediately to answer the call. GM quickly went to work on the Chevy Camaro and Pontiac Firebird, and even struggling American Motors started developing the Javelin and the AMX, a surprisingly competent two-seater. Little remembered, however, is the fact that Plymouth actually beat Ford to the market by two weeks with its '64 Barracuda.

Even though the Mustang had the allure of being a poor man's Corvette, the Barracuda was seen exactly for what it was—a Valiant with bucket

seats and improved styling. The Mustang buyer could seemingly order his machine with a million different options; the Barracuda came only with the dependable (but uninspiring) Slant Six or the 273 2-barrel V8. Some early cars even had both Barracuda and Valiant badges on them—not exactly the hot ticket for Walter Mitty types.

By 1965 the United States was overcome by Mustang mania. Ford had the plants going day and night to try to keep up with demand. Not much was new in the Mustang camp in 1965: the 260 was replaced by 2- and 4-barrel versions of the 289, and the fastback model mentioned earlier was added. Also, the gauge cluster was redesigned to help the car mask its Falcon roots. The GT package stayed the same for those who wanted a sportier ride with better handling and quicker steering. But the true crushing blow to the competition—which now included the almighty Corvette Sting Ray—was the Shelby Mustang GT350.

The GT350 was a race-prepped version of the Mustang, created by Carroll Shelby in his tiny facility at Los Angeles International Airport. The engine was worked over with Tri-Y exhaust headers, an aluminum high-rise intake and Holley carb, and a high-lift cam, bringing horsepower from 271 to 306. Shelby then had his engineers rework the suspension and brakes, remove the backseat, and install a functional fiberglass hood. The resulting automobiles terrorized the B/Production ranks of the SCCA (Sports Car Club of America).

Chrysler, realizing the error of its marketing ways with the Barracuda, began improving that package. For 1965 it released the Formula S version, which offered larger-diameter torsion bars for increased roll stiffness, a front stabilizer bar, heavy-duty rear springs with 6 leaves instead of the standard 4½, and stiffer shocks.

Powering the Formula S was a warmed-over version of the 273 with a 4-barrel carburetor, a mechanical-lifter camshaft, and a tricky high-flowing single exhaust (there wasn't room for true duals). In an October 1964 road test, *Car and Driver* called the new model "everything you'd like it to be." The Commando 273 V8 was a big step up in the horsepower department, thanks to its 10.5:1 compression ratio (up from 8.8:1), improved valve timing, and better cam lift. The standard gear ratio was the 3.23, plenty snappy for a small car.

Top: Ford's Mustang grew in size in 1967 and its engine bay was enlarged so it could accommodate the big-block FE family of engines (390, 427, 428). Above: The '67 Camaro became a collectible almost the moment it was released. It was available with hundreds of options, and it is almost certain that no two were exactly alike. This one features both the "Super Sport" and the "Rally Sport" packages.

CHEVROLET CAMARO

1967

Cu. In.	302	327	350
Bore (in.)	4.00	4.00	4.00
Stroke (in.)	3.00	3.25	3.48
Compression	11.00:1	10.00:1	10.25:1
Induction	1x4 bbl.	1x4 bbl.	1x4 bbl.
Horsepower/RPM	290/5800	275/4800	295/4800
Torque (lbs.-ft.)/RPM	290/4200	355/3200	380/3200

1967 (cont.)

Cu. In.	396	
Bore (in.)	4.094	
Stroke (in.)	3.76	
Compression	10.25:1	11.00:1
Induction	1x4 bbl.	1x4 bbl.
Horsepower/RPM	325/4800	375/5600
Torque (lbs.-ft.)/RPM	410/3200	415/3600

1968

Cu. In.	302	327	350
Bore (in.)	4.00	4.00	4.00
Stroke (in.)	3.00	3.25	3.48
Compression	11.00:1	10.00:1	10.25:1
Induction	1x4 bbl.	1x4 bbl.	1x4 bbl.
Horsepower/RPM	290/5800	275/4800	295/4800
Torque (lbs.-ft.)/RPM	290/4200	355/3200	380/3200

1968 (cont.)

Cu. In.	396		
Bore (in.)	4.094		
Stroke (in.)	3.76		
Compression	10.25:1	11.00:1	11.00:1
Induction	1x4 bbl.	1x4 bbl.	1x4 bbl.
Horsepower/RPM	325/4800	350/5200	375/5600
Torque (lbs.-ft.)/RPM	410/3200	415/3400	415/3600

1969

Cu. In.	302	350
Bore (in.)	4.00	4.00
Stroke (in.)	3.00	3.48
Compression	11.00:1	10.25:1
Induction	1x4 bbl.	1x4 bbl.
Horsepower/RPM	290/5800	300/4800
Torque (lbs.-ft.)/RPM	290/4200	380/3200

1969 (cont.)

Cu. In.	396		
Bore (in.)	4.094		
Stroke (in.)	3.76		
Compression	10.25:1	11.00:1	11.00:1
Induction	1x4 bbl.	1x4 bbl.	1x4 bbl.
Horsepower/RPM	325/4800	350/5200	375/5600
Torque (lbs.-ft.)/RPM	410/3200	415/3400	415/3600

1970

Cu. In.	350	402	
Bore (in.)	4.00	4.126	
Stroke (in.)	3.48	3.76	
Compression	11.00:1	11.00:1	11.00:1
Induction	1x4 bbl.	1x4 bbl.	1x4 bbl.
Horsepower/RPM	360/6000	350/5200	375/5600
Torque (lbs.-ft.)/RPM	380/4000	415/3400	415/3600

1971

Cu. In.	350	402
Bore (in.)	4.00	4.126
Stroke (in.)	3.48	3.76
Compression	9.00:1	9.00:1
Induction	1x4 bbl.	1x4 bbl.
Horsepower/RPM	330/5600	300/4800
Torque (lbs.-ft.)/RPM	360/4000	360/4000

1972

Cu. In.	350	402
Bore (in.)	4.00	4.126
Stroke (in.)	3.48	3.76
Compression	9.00:1	8.50:1
Induction	1x4 bbl.	1x4 bbl.
Horsepower/RPM	255/5600	240/4400
Torque (lbs.-ft.)/RPM	280/4000	345/3200

The Camaro Z/28 (left) was the only Chevy to receive the 290-horsepower 302. The '67 Camaro (right) received the 350 V8 two years before the Corvette and still uses a version of it today.

Better Living Through Cubic Inches

When word leaked to Ford that the soon-to-be-released '67 Chevrolet Camaro would pack the punch of a 396, Mustang's planners immediately went to work shoehorning the 390 into the tight confines of the Mustang engine compartment. The engineers relocated the shock towers and broadened the pony's engine bay. With little room to spare, the heavy, massive 390 was stuffed in and was available as an option from the beginning of the '67 model year—some three months ahead of the 396 Camaro.

Because of the cramped underhood space, the exhaust system was more restrictive in the Mustang than in mid- and full-size Fords. Still, the 390 made 320 horsepower and enough torque to make people forget about the terrific high performance 289. It gave the Mustang quicker acceleration from 0 to 60 mph, and made it faster through the quarter-mile, plus it cost $169.74 less than its smaller friend, which died with the 1967 model year.

Far fewer 396-powered Camaros (5,141) than Mustangs were sold that year, partly because the big block wasn't available until three months into the model year, but their impact was more widely felt. While the 390 Mustang was competitive with the 325-hp Camaro, it was no match for the 375-horse L78. It was this car, in fact, that inspired Ford to build 427 and 428 Mustangs starting in 1968.

The Camaro was Chevrolet's entry into the ponycar wars and, like the Mustang and Barracuda, was based on a compact car—in this case the Chevy Nova. Like the Mustang, the Camaro could be ordered in a multitude of trim levels—base, Rally Sport (RS), Super Sport (SS), a combination RS/SS—and with a plethora of engine choices. It sold exceedingly well, with 195,765 going out the door in its maiden campaign.

The combination of the Camaro Z/28, driver Mark Donohue, and owner Roger Penske was near unbeatable from 1967 to 1969, winning an astounding twenty-one races and two championships. In 1970 Donohue and Penske were lured to the American Motors team to race Javelins.

Camaro Z/28—The Giant Killer

In 1967 Chevrolet's need for a powerful 5-liter car that accelerated like a dragster and handled like a slot car sired the Camaro Z/28, one of the true Davids in a field awash with Goliaths.

Because Detroit was churning out small sedans like the Dodge Dart and Ford Falcon, and ponycars like the Mustang and Barracuda, it was only natural that someone was going to start a race series for them. That someone turned out to be the SCCA, which thought up the idea of the Trans-Am series. Two classes of cars were permitted: under-2-liter sedans (123 cubic inches)—ideal for imports—and over 2 liters for cars with a maximum wheelbase of 116 cubic inches and a minimum weight of 2,800 pounds.

The first race was run in 1966 at Sebring and nine over-2-liter cars showed up—three Mustangs, three Barracudas, two Corvairs, and a Dart. While durability was proving to be a bit of a problem, the action was attracting the attention of some big-name drivers. For the fourth race, four well-known stock car drivers—Curtis Turner, Richard Petty, David Pearson, and Wendell Scott—participated. Those who looked closely saw that three of the eight Mustang teams were racing under Carroll Shelby's colors, indicating clear factory support from Ford. This certainly helped as it won four of the seven races, thus giving Mustang the first of the three championships

it would win (1966, 1967, 1970) during the muscle car era.

For 1967 the series expanded to twelve races and the amount of factory participation also increased. Three Cougar teams joined the fray, and Chevrolet entered its new Camaro.

Chevy found itself in a predicament because the T-A cubic-inch limit was 305 cubic inches. Its 283 was too small, its 327 too large. The answer was an old hot-rodder trick. Put the 283 crank in the 327 block and come up with a 302. Chevrolet built 602 of these screamers for the street, and they took the ponycar world by storm. They came with radical solid-lifter camshafts, the Corvette's fuelie heads, an aluminum intake, and an 800 cfm Holley carb. The suspension was also revised.

At the track, Chevy employed the owner-driver team of Roger Penske and Mark Donohue. While this team worked the new combo to three victories in twelve races in 1967, they were nearly unbeatable in 1968. The Penske-Sunoco blue-and-gold Camaro won ten of thirteen races that year, including eight in a row.

For 1969 the Penske-Donohue team was less dominant, but only by the slightest of margins. The team won eight of the twelve races, with Ford winning the other four with its new Boss 302 Mustangs.

Although it arrived at the market months after its Camaro cousin, many muscle car aficionados feel that the Pontiac Firebird (right and below) was a better car because of its extra development time. While it didn't have as many engine offerings as the Camaro, it did quite well in 1967 with the 326 H.O. and 325-hp 400.

The Firebird Takes Wing

While the Firebird was also a success, Pontiac general manager John Delorean originally wanted nothing to do with it. He was convinced that the division could do better with an inexpensive two-seater based on the Banshee show car. It wasn't until the last minute, when GM forced the four-seat F-body on him, that Pontiac went to work on the Firebird.

Although this delay caused the Firebird to arrive on the scene three months later than the Camaro, it also allowed Pontiac engineers the time they needed to refine the Firebird.

Because the outside dimensions of the 400 are the same as those of the 326, Pontiac engineers had no problem fitting the 400 in the Firebird. From the very beginning, the Firebird could be ordered with the potent Ram Air 400 V8. Because of a GM edict that passenger cars not be sold with more than 1 horsepower for every 10 pounds of vehicle weight, the RA 400 was underrated at 325 horsepower. In actuality, it was almost the same engine that was rated at 360 horsepower in the GTO. The main differences were a more restrictive exhaust system and a kink in the linkage on the Quadrajet 4-barrel that didn't allow the secondaries to open fully. Straighten the linkage, and you'd gain back much of the lost 25 horsepower. With 3.90 gears, this was good enough for low 14-second performance in the quarter-mile at about 100 mph.

This wasn't the only high-performance Firebird you could order in 1967. If you wanted to go fast without the headaches of high insurance, you could order the 326 H.O. with 285 horsepower.

The ponycar market was so explosive that in 1967 even Mercury got into the act with the new Cougar. Larger, heavier, and aimed at a more up-scale buyer than the Mustang it was based on, the Cougar could be ordered with a leather interior, a wood-rim steering wheel, and, for the performance-minded, the 390 with its 427 lbs.-ft. of torque.

A Dangerous Fish

For 1967 Plymouth completely restyled its Barracuda—quite successfully if you believed Car and Driver's claim that it was "unquestionably the best looking car out of Detroit in 1967."

Certainly, the styling was fresh. While the fastback was still around, the wraparound glass was replaced by a more traditional steel roof blending

---

PONTIAC

1967

Cu. In.	326	400
Bore (in.)	3.72	4.12
Stroke (in.)	3.75	3.75
Compression	10.50:1	10.75:1
Induction	1x4 bbl.	1x4 bbl.
Horsepower/RPM	285/5000	325/5200
Torque (lbs.-ft.)/RPM	359/3200	410/3600

1968

Cu. In.	350	400	
Bore (in.)	3.88	4.12	
Stroke (in.)	3.75	3.75	
Compression	10.50:1	10.75:1	
Induction	1x4 bbl.	1x4 bbl.	
Horsepower/RPM	320/5100	330/4800	335/5000
Torque (lbs.-ft.)/RPM	380/3200	430/3300	430/3400

1969

Cu. In.	350	400	
Bore (in.)	3.88	4.12	
Stroke (in.)	3.75	3.75	
Compression	10.50:1	10.75:1	
Induction	1x4 bbl.	1x4 bbl.	
Horsepower/RPM	325/5100	330/4800	335/5000
Torque (lbs.-ft.)/RPM	380/3200	430/3300	430/3400

1969 (cont.)

Cu. In.	400
Bore (in.)	4.12
Stroke (in.)	3.75
Compression	10.75:1
Induction	1x4 bbl.
Horsepower/RPM	345/5400
Torque (lbs.-ft.)/RPM	440/3700

1970

Cu. In.	400		
Bore (in.)	4.12		
Stroke (in.)	3.75		
Compression	10.00:1	10.25:1	10.50:1
Induction	1x4 bbl.	1x4 bbl.	1x4 bbl.
Horsepower/RPM	330/4800	335/4800	370/5500
Torque (lbs.-ft.)/RPM	445/2900	430/3000	445/3900

1971

Cu. In.	400	455	
Bore (in.)	4.12	4.15	
Stroke (in.)	3.75	4.21	
Compression	8.20:1	8.20:1	8.40:1
Induction	1x4 bbl.	1x4 bbl.	1x4 bbl.
Horsepower/RPM	300/4800	325/4400	335/4800
Torque (lbs.-ft.)/RPM	400/2400	455/3200	480/3600

1972

Cu. In.	400	455
Bore (in.)	4.12	4.15
Stroke (in.)	3.75	4.21
Compression	8.20:1	8.40:1
Induction	1x4 bbl.	1x4 bbl.
Horsepower/RPM	250/4400	300/4000
Torque (lbs.-ft.)/RPM	325/3200	415/3200

1973

Cu. In.	400	455	
Bore (in.)	4.12	4.15	
Stroke (in.)	3.75	4.21	
Compression	8.00:1	8.00:1	8.40:1
Induction	1x4 bbl.	1x4 bbl.	1x4 bbl.
Horsepower/RPM	230/4400	250/4000	310/4000
Torque (lbs.-ft.)/RPM	325/3200	370/2800	390/3600

1974

Cu. In.	400	455
Bore (in.)	4.12	4.15
Stroke (in.)	3.75	4.21
Compression	8.00:1	8.40:1
Induction	1x4 bbl.	1x4 bbl.
Horsepower/RPM	225/4400	290/4000
Torque (lbs.-ft.)/RPM	330/2800	390/3600

Above left: The '67 Barracuda could be had with a 383, but these engines were rare, expensive, and not even-tempered. More folks opted for the more civilized 273 with the 4-barrel carburetor. With 235 horsepower, the 273 made for a spirited ponycar that was insurance-company and gas-mileage friendly. Above right: Aimed at the upscale end of the ponycar market, the '67 Mercury Cougar had a longer wheelbase and more luxurious accoutrements than its Mustang cousin. Right or wrong, more than one magazine at the time called it "America's Jaguar." The top engine was the Mustang's 390; the high-performance 289, however, came only in the 'Stang. Only one body style, a two-door coupe, was available.

Among the unusual features of the '67 Barracuda interior were a speedometer that was numbered 1, 2, 3, etc., instead of 10, 20, 30, etc., and a very small tachometer in the center of the gauge cluster (which Plymouth engineers called a "Performance Indicator").

into the bodywork. There was also a notchback version available for the first time. There was an all-new interior to go with the clean sheet metal. And while it wasn't easy, the engineers managed to stuff a 280-horsepower version of the torquey 383 under the hood.

This gave you plenty of neck-snapping torque and a car that could definitely run with the 320-horse Mustang and 325-horse SS396 Camaro. There is, however, some confusion as to how many 'Cudas were built. According to Al Kirschenbaum, the following numbers from Chrysler Historical (the archival arm of the Chrysler Corp.) are the most accurate of the various accounts that have been released over the years: 1,841 for 1967; 1,270 for 1968; 1,179 for 1969.

It should be noted that power steering was offered on these cars for the first time in 1969. If you're looking for exclusivity, buy a '69 383 convertible (330 hp, 425 lbs.-ft. of torque). Only seven were built with the manual transmission and just ten with automatic.

Also in 1969, Plymouth shocked the muscle car world by building 340 'Cudas with the mon-

strous 440 V8 from its GTX. This engine was almost more motor than the compact-based car could handle. With 375 horsepower and 480 lbs.-ft. of torque, it had drag racing aficionados dancing in the staging lanes, even though a 4-speed was not available.

Neither the 383 nor the 440 'Cuda was a paragon of automotive virtue on the street. If a strong-running, easy-living highway star was more your speed, you could opt for the 275-horse 340 V8, a brand-new engine introduced in 1968. It was the best small-bore engine Chrysler ever developed. A 6000-rpm small block right from the factory, it could propel the lightweight Barracuda to 14.2-second ETs on street tires.

In 1968 Ford had upped the ante with 427 and 428 engines for the Mustang and Cougar. The 427 was a detuned version of its low-riser engine. In the Mustang and Cougar, it came with a hydraulic-lifter camshaft, a single Holley 4-barrel, and an automatic transmission. Still, its 390 horsepower was nothing to scoff at.

But the 427 was destined to be just a stepping stone for the now-legendary 428 Cobra Jet,

DODGE CHALLENGER/PLYMOUTH 'CUDA

1965

Cu. In.	273	
Bore (in.)	3.63	
Stroke (in.)	3.31	
Compression	10.50:1	
Induction	1x4 bbl.	
Horsepower/RPM	235/5200	
Torque (lbs.-ft.)/RPM	280/4000	

1966

Cu. In.	273
Bore (in.)	3.63
Stroke (in.)	3.31
Compression	10.50:1
Induction	1x4 bbl.
Horsepower/RPM	235/5200
Torque (lbs.-ft.)/RPM	280/4000

1967

Cu. In.	273	383
Bore (in.)	3.63	4.25
Stroke (in.)	3.31	3.38
Compression	10.50:1	10.00:1
Induction	1x4 bbl.	1x4 bbl.
Horsepower/RPM	235/5200	280/4200
Torque (lbs.-ft.)/RPM	280/4000	400/2400

1968

Cu. In.	340	383
Bore (in.)	4.04	4.25
Stroke (in.)	3.31	3.38
Compression	10.50:1	10.00:1
Induction	1x4 bbl.	1x4 bbl
Horsepower/RPM	275/5000	300/4400
Torque (lbs.-ft.)/RPM	340/3200	400/2400

1969

Cu. In.	340	383	440
Bore (in.)	4.04	4.25	4.32
Stroke (in.)	3.31	3.38	3.75
Compression	10.50:1	10.00:1	10.10:1
Induction	1x4 bbl.	1x4 bbl.	1x4 bbl.
Horsepower/RPM	275/5000	330/4400	375/4600
Torque (lbs.-ft.)/RPM	340/3200	425/3400	480/3200

1970

Cu. In.	340		383
Bore (in.)	4.04		4.25
Stroke (in.)	3.31		3.38
Compression	10.50:1		9.50:1
Induction	1x4 bbl.	3x2 bbl.	1x4 bbl.
Horsepower/RPM	275/5000	290/5000	335/5200
Torque (lbs.-ft.)/RPM	340/3200	340/3200	425/3400

1970 (cont.)

Cu. In.	440		426
Bore (in.)	4.32		4.25
Stroke (in.)	3.75		3.75
Compression	9.70:1	10.50:1	10.25:1
Induction	1x4 bbl.	3x2 bbl.	2x4 bbl.
Horsepower/RPM	375/4600	390/4700	425/5000
Torque (lbs.-ft.)/RPM	480/3200	490/3200	490/4000

1971

Cu. In.	340	383
Bore (in.)	4.04	4.25
Stroke (in.)	3.31	3.38
Compression	10.50:1	8.50:1
Induction	1x4 bbl.	1x4 bbl.
Horsepower/RPM	275/5000	300/4800
Torque (lbs.-ft.)/RPM	340/3200	410/3400

1971 (cont.)

Cu. In.	440		426
Bore (in.)	4.32		4.25
Stroke (in.)	3.75		3.75
Compression	9.70:1	10.50:1	10.25:1
Induction	1x4 bbl.	3x2 bbl.	2x4 bbl.
Horsepower/RPM	370/4600	385/4700	425/5000
Torque (lbs. ft.)/RPM	480/3200	490/3200	490/4000

1972

Cu. In.	340
Bore (in.)	4.04
Stroke (in.)	3.31
Compression	8.50:1
Induction	1x4 bbl.
Horsepower/RPM	240/4800
Torque (lbs.-ft.)/RPM	290/3600

1973

Cu. In.	340
Bore (in.)	4.04
Stroke (in.)	3.31
Compression	8.50:1
Induction	1x4 bbl.
Horsepower/RPM	240/4800
Torque (lbs.-ft.)/RPM	295/3600

1974

Cu. In.	360
Bore (in.)	4.00
Stroke (in.)	3.58
Compression	8.40:1
Induction	1x4 bbl.
Horsepower/RPM	245/4800
Torque (lbs.-ft.)/RPM	320/3600

Three Holley 2-barrel carbs gave the 340 engine more horsepower (290 vs. 275) than its single 4-barrel stablemates. The three-deuce mill was an AAR 'Cuda and Trans-Am Challenger exclusive and lasted only one model year—1970.

which debuted on April 1, 1968. It was the automotive equivalent of an atom bomb. *Hot Rod* magazine called it "the fastest Pure Stock in the history of man."

The new Cobra Jet (CJ) was available throughout the Ford and Mercury lineups, replacing the venerable 427. The 428 CJ was based on the 428 Police Interceptor block, but with big-valve 427 heads, 10.6:1 compression, a bumpy hydraulic-lifter cam, and a 735 cfm Holley 4V on a cast-iron intake. Underrated at 335 horsepower, it won its class at the Winternationals the first time out. *Hot Rod*'s test results, as seen in Ford's print ads in the spring of 1968, were 0–60 in 5.9 and 13.56 at 106.64 mph in the quarter-mile.

The year 1968 also saw the debut of an American Motors entry—the Javelin—into the fray. Based on the AMX show car, this vehicle had the typical long-hood, short-deck ponycar look. Its underpinnings were typical, antiquated AMC pieces, but somehow the engineers made it all work very well. Outside, the Javelin was a winner with its

Aerodynamic duo

Front: Camaro SS Sport Coupe. Rear: Corvette Sting Ray Coupe.

They're two of a kind. The fantastic, low-slung Corvette Sting Ray. And Camaro, The Hugger, the only car that comes even close. In styling, in handling, in performance. Both are aerodynamic from nose to deck, with Astro Ventilation, full door-glass styling, bucket seats, refined suspension and 327-cu.-in. standard V8s. You can order Vettes all the way up to 435 hp in a 427-cu.-in. Turbo-Jet V8. Camaros score almost as high: Cubes — 396. Horses — 325. Corvette's a tough act to follow. Buckle up a Camaro and see what we've done for an encore.

'68 Camaro Corvette

semi-fastback roofline, ventless side glass, and flush door handles. Also, its interior was completely unlike that of most AMC cars.

Three V8s were optional in the Javelin: a 290 cubic incher for the economy-minded, a 280-horse 343 4-barrel for the more sporting-inclined, and by midyear the 390 4-barrel, which debuted in the production AMX.

While most muscle car fans erroneously believe that the AMX is a two-seat version of the Javelin, the opposite is actually true—the Javelin was a stretched version of the AMX. American Motors insiders knew that they couldn't afford to build two separate sporty cars, so they decided to forge ahead with the Javelin. When Robert Evans became chairman of AMC, he gave the go-ahead to build both, so long as they shared many parts.

Left: For the 1968 model year Chevrolet tried to enhance the Camaro's image by linking it to the new, radically styled Corvette, which was based on the 1965 Mako Shark II dream car.

Left: After 1970 American Motors killed the two-seat AMX and made the designation an option on the restyled '71 Javelin. This car boasts the unusual Pierre Cardin interior package, which was offered on the Javelin and AMX in 1972 and 1973. This package included brightly colored stripes across the front and rear seats and the roof, plus the designer's trademark "PC" logo on the doors Right: The Javelin AMX could be ordered with a fiberglass cowl induction hood. A flap on the air cleaner lid allowed a charge of cold air to reach the carburetor.

The 290 V8 was standard in the AMX, while the 343 and the 390 were offered as options. The 390—which was basically a bored and stroked 343 with big-valve heads and forged-steel internals—was rated at 315 horsepower. This made for excellent performance in both the Javelin and the AMX, and for the first time performance-minded Americans were seen shopping at AMC dealerships, which had long been perceived as the domain of wimps, nerds, and the frugal-minded. Magazine ads implored potential buyers to "Test Drag a Javelin."

AMC backed both of these cars with a wide assortment of dealer-installed and over-the-counter goodies. It was easy for the Javelin or AMX buyer to drive away from the showroom with a machine that was considerably meaner than the stock version of either vehicle.

Both the Camaro and the Firebird were basically carryovers with minor face-lifts for 1968.

AMERICAN MOTORS AMX AND JAVELIN

1968

Cu. In.	343	390
Bore (in.)	4.08	4.17
Stroke (in.)	3.28	3.57
Compression	10.20:1	10.20:1
Induction	1x4 bbl.	1x4 bbl.
Horsepower/RPM	280/4800	315/4600
Torque (lbs.-ft.)/RPM	365/3000	425/3200

1969

Cu. In.	343	390	
Bore (in.)	4.08	4.17	
Stroke (in.)	3.28	3.57	
Compression	10.20:1	10.20:1	12.30:1*
Induction	1x4 bbl.	1x4 bbl.	2x4 bbl.
Horsepower/RPM	280/4800	315/4600	340
Torque (lbs.-ft.)/RPM	365/3000	425/3200	not rated
*AMX S/S only			

1970

Cu. In.	360	390
Bore (in.)	4.08	4.17
Stroke (in.)	3.34	3.57
Compression	10.00:1	10.00:1
Induction	1x4 bbl.	1x4 bbl.
Horsepower/RPM	290/4800	325/5000
Torque (lbs.-ft.)/RPM	395/3200	420/3200

1971

Cu. In.	360	401
Bore (in.)	4.08	4.17
Stroke (in.)	3.34	3.68
Compression	8.50:1	9.50:1*
Induction	1x4 bbl.	1x4 bbl.
Horsepower/RPM	285/4800	330/5000
Torque (lbs.-ft.)/RPM	390/3200	430/3400
*Early production had 10.20:1 c.r.		

1972

Cu. In.	360	401
Bore (in.)	4.08	4.17
Stroke (in.)	3.34	3.68
Compression	8.50:1	8.50:1
Induction	1x4 bbl.	1x4 bbl.
Horsepower/RPM	220/4400	255/4600
Torque (lbs.-ft.)/RPM	315/3100	345/3300

1973

Cu. In.	360	401
Bore (in.)	4.08	4.17
Stroke (in.)	3.34	3.68
Compression	8.50:1	8.50:1
Induction	1x4 bbl.	1x4 bbl.
Horsepower/RPM	220/4400	255/4600
Torque (lbs.-ft.)/RPM	315/3100	345/3300

1974

Cu. In.	360	401
Bore (in.)	4.08	4.17
Stroke (in.)	3.34	3.68
Compression	8.50:1	8.50:1*
Induction	1x4 bbl.	1x4 bbl.
Horsepower/RPM	220/4400	255/4600
Torque (lbs.-ft.)/RPM	315/3100	345/3300
*Lowered to 8.25 early in model year.		

American Motors' two-seat AMX, which only lasted from 1968 to 1970, was as wild as anything the Big Three were producing at the time. This AMX features "Big Bad Orange" paint.

Chevrolet played the Camaro off the dramatically styled new Corvette in its advertising, touting them as the "Aerodynamic Duo" in one ad. Another called the Camaro "The Closest Thing to a Corvette Yet."

In the Firebird camp, refinement was the name of the game, with the 350 H.O. the only new engine. Horsepower was up to 330 with the 400 (335 with Ram Air).

Later in the year, the Ram Air II showed up with 345 ponies and 445 lbs.-ft. of torque. This was a very serious machine, thanks to a hotter cam and better cylinder heads.

Doin' Fine in '69

Like the Vietnam War, the ponycar conflict quickly got out of control as the Big Three and little AMC did their best to outgun each other in the showroom and on race tracks. While the AMX and Javelin were largely carryovers with refinements for 1969, the Mustang, Camaro, and Firebird got major face-lifts—not to mention outrageous engine transplants.

The Mustang was pretty much all new in 1969: bigger, more aggressive, and better-looking than ever. While its wheelbase remained much the same, the car was longer and wider, and its design

philosophy changed. It went from a cute car to all-out warrior, especially in Mach 1 trim. While the GT was still available, it would not be for long.

The Mach 1 'Stang was Ford's answer to the Camaro SS. Though its base engine was the uninspired 250-horse 351 Windsor (new for 1969), a 290-horse 4-barrel version was optional, as was a 320-horsepower 390 and two versions of the king-hell 428.

The first 428 was the Cobra Jet, a virtual carry-over from the late-1968 engine. But if you ordered the 3.91 or 4.30:1 rear axle ratio for $6.53, you got the Super Cobra Jet package, which gave your

Left: The new-for-1969 Mustang Mach I (top) was an instant sales sensation, making the previous GT superfluous. For 1970 the American Motors AMX (bottom) received a new grille and hood design. The flat-black hood paint treatment was called the Shadow Mask option. Right: The '69 Camaro was the most successful to date; whether this was because of this advertising or in spite of it is open to debate. This was sixties chic, Madison Avenue–style.

FORD MUSTANG/MERCURY COUGAR

1965

Cu. In.	289
Bore (in.)	4.00
Stroke (in.)	2.87
Compression	10.50:1
Induction	1x4 bbl.
Horsepower/RPM	271/6000
Torque (lbs.-ft.)/RPM	312/3400

1966

Cu. In.	289
Bore (in.)	4.00
Stroke (in.)	2.87
Compression	10.50:1
Induction	1x4 bbl.
Horsepower/RPM	271/6000
Torque (lbs.-ft.)/RPM	312/3400

1967

Cu. In.	289	390
Bore (in.)	4.00	4.05
Stroke (in.)	2.87	3.78
Compression	10.50:1	10.50:1
Induction	1x4 bbl.	1x4 bbl.
Horsepower/RPM	271/6000	320/4800
Torque (lbs.-ft.)/RPM	312/3400	427/3200

1968

Cu. In.	390	427	428
Bore (in.)	4.05	4.23	4.13
Stroke (in.)	3.78	3.78	3.98
Compression	10.50:1	10.90:1	10.70:1
Induction	1x4 bbl.	1x4 bbl.	1x4 bbl.
Horsepower/RPM	325/4800	390/4600	335/5600
Torque (lbs.-ft.)/RPM	427/3200	460/3200	445/3400

1969

Cu. In.	302	351	390
Bore (in.)	4.00	4.00	4.05
Stroke (in.)	3.00	3.50	3.78
Compression	10.50:1	10.70:1	10.50:1
Induction	1x4 bbl.	1x4 bbl.	1x4 bbl.
Horsepower/RPM	290/5800	290/4800	320/4600
Torque (lbs.-ft.)/RPM	290/4300	385/3200	427/3200

1969 (cont.)

Cu. In.	428	429
Bore (in.)	4.13	4.36
Stroke (in.)	3.98	3.59
Compression	10.60:1	10.50:1
Induction	1x4 bbl.	1x4 bbl.
Horsepower/RPM	335/5200	375/5200
Torque (lbs.-ft.)/RPM	440/3400	450/3400

1970

Cu. In.	302	351
Bore (in.)	4.00	4.00
Stroke (in.)	3.00	3.50
Compression	10.50:1	11.00:1
Induction	1x4 bbl.	1x4 bbl.
Horsepower/RPM	290/5800	300/5400
Torque (lbs.-ft.)/RPM	290/4300	380/3400

1970 (cont.)

Cu. In.	428	429
Bore (in.)	4.13	4.36
Stroke (in.)	3.98	3.59
Compression	10.60:1	10.50:1
Induction	1x4 bbl.	1x4 bbl.
Horsepower/RPM	335/5200	375/5200
Torque (lbs.-ft.)/RPM	440/3400	450/3400

1971

Cu. In.	351	351*
Bore (In.)	4.00	4.00
Stroke (in.)	3.50	3.50
Compression	10.70:1	11.00:1
Induction	1x4 bbl.	1x4 bbl.
Horsepower/RPM	285/5400	330/5400
Torque (lbs.-ft.)/RPM	370/3400	370/4000

* Boss

1971 (cont.)

Cu. In.	429	
Bore (in.)	4.36	
Stroke (in.)	3.59	
Compression	11.30:1	
Induction	1x4 bbl.	
Horsepower/RPM	370/5400	375/5600
Torque (lbs.-ft.)/RPM	450/3400	450/3400

1972

Cu. In.	351	
Bore (in.)	4.00	
Stroke (in.)	3.50	
Compression	8.60:1	8.80:1
Induction	1x4 bbl.	1x4 bbl.
Horsepower/RPM	266/5400	275/6000
Torque (lbs.-ft.)/RPM	301/3600	286/3800

1973

Cu. In.	351
Bore (in.)	4.00
Stroke (in.)	3.50
Compression	8.60:1
Induction	1x4 bbl.
Horsepower/RPM	266/5400
Torque (lbs.-ft.)/RPM	301/3600

428 (among other things) 427 LeMans-style connecting rods, an external engine oil cooler, and a beefier crankshaft. This option was the bargain of the decade.

What really made the Mach 1 special was its packaging. A flat-black scooped hood was standard, as were side stripes, a flip-open gas cap, and Mach 1 nomenclature. Combined with the new styling of the fastback, with its built-in side scoops and ducktail rear spoiler, this made the Mach I look like it was going 100 mph even when it was sitting still. Opting for the Ram Air package gave you the industry's first "shaker" hood. The air scoop was mounted directly to the carburetor and stuck up through a hole in the hood.

The Mustang also got an all-new interior in 1969, one far superior to any previously offered. Mach 1 sales took off (over seventy thousand cars were sold), though overall Mustang sales fell. While some experts feel that this was due to the fact that the car kept getting larger and wasn't true to its small-car roots, it cannot be overlooked that the market had expanded to seven models where there had been only two just three years prior.

If you wanted the ultimate Mustang, you had to find a dealership with a Boss 429 in stock. To legalize the 429 semi-Hemi engine for its NASCAR Torinos and Cyclones, Ford had Kar Kraft of Brighton, Michigan, build 857 Mustangs (and two Cougars) with a detuned version of this race mill.

The heart of the Boss 429 was its aluminum Hemi-type cylinder heads. Its massive valves were fed by a relatively tiny 735 cfm Holley 4-barrel on an aluminum intake. Although the Boss came undercammed from the factory, there was potential for astounding performance if you had the money.

To mark its entry into the SCCA's Trans-Am series, Pontiac introduced the aptly named Firebird Trans-Am. Pontiac has paid a fee to the SCCA for every such 'Bird ever built; thanks to the car's sales success, this royalty has totaled millions of dollars.

In 1969 Ford also released it answer to the Z/28. Engineers put the canted-valve cylinder heads from the upcoming 351 Cleveland power plant on the 302 block. The result, known as the Boss 302, was every bit the high-winding banshee that the Chevy was. It came wrapped in a graphics package created by designer Larry Shinoda (of '63 and '68 Corvette fame), and it featured side stripes, front and rear spoilers, rear window slats, and filled-in side scoops.

General Motors' F-body twins both received major face-lifts in 1969. While the Pontiac's was terrific, the '69 Camaro is now considered the model by which all others are judged. Sales shot up from 235,147 to 243,085, though the engines were basically carryovers. If you found yourself

long on cash, you could opt for the L89 aluminum cylinder heads, which chopped quite a bit of weight off your front end and even more from your wallet—a whopping $710.95. (To put this in perspective, consider that the base price of a V8 Camaro was $2,727 and the L78 option cost only $316.)

The Firebird's face-lift was more evolutionary than revolutionary. But the Firebird that made everyone take notice was the Trans Am.

Despite its name, the T/A was never eligible to compete in the race series of the same name because its engine was the 400-cube Ram Air V8 (now known as Ram Air III)—there was a 305-cube limit. In competition, the Firebirds were eligible to use Chevy's 302 because Canadian-built Firebirds

had it as an option, a move that left Pontiac enthusiasts on the verge of tears. On the street, however, the RA III left them with tears of joy.

The RA III's forward-facing dual hood scoops, which were opened and closed by the driver, fed cold air to a 4-barrel Quadrajet carb. With 10.75:1 compression, this engine was rated at 335 ponies. The 345-horse Ram Air IV, which used different heads, a hotter cam, an aluminum intake, and round port exhaust manifolds, was optional.

Rounding out the visual package were twin blue stripes running across the top of the white body from front to back, functional side scoops, and a salami-slicer rear spoiler mounted to the decklid. The taillight panel was painted the same blue as the body stripes.

To improve handling, quicker variable ratio power steering was standard, as were heavy-duty springs, staggered shocks, a 1-inch front sway bar, and 14-inch wheels. Only 697 T/As—eight of them convertibles—were built in the marque's first year.

Plymouth's ads for 1969 were getting more and more psychedelic; the one for its 'Cuda 340 looked like it was designed by someone on LSD. The car had eyes, it was belching fire and smoke, and it was passing a drag strip Christmas tree that was as twisted as the art itself.

The Dodge Challenger T/A (above) was not for the bashful. It was painted attention-grabbing colors and featured loud, side-exiting exhaust pipes. Power for the T/A came from a worked-over 340 (right) that benefited from a functional fiberglass hood that fed air to three Holley 2-barrel carbs. The interior (below) could be ordered with the Rallye gauge cluster, which gave you (among other things) a tachometer, clock, and 150-mph speedometer.

The Last Waltz

For muscle car fans, the year 1970 was the summit of the horsepower wars. Things never got this wild again. New ponycars appeared on the scene, but they often went wanting for buyers.

Take the redesigned Plymouth Barracuda and its Dodge Challenger stablemate. Instead of continuing them on the compact A-body platform, Chrysler engineers came up with a downsized version of the midsize B-body chassis (dubbed the E-body). Although this chassis was exceptional styling-wise and the larger, wider engine compartments made fitting the Street Hemi and the 440 Six-Packs as easy as shooting fish in a barrel, buyers resisted.

The situation was similar over at General Motors. While the Camaro and Firebird were all new and featured styling that was compared to that of Ferraris in some of the buff books, it took years for them to catch on the way the '67–'69 models did.

As far as performance was concerned, nothing could match the '70 models. 'Cudas and Challengers, for example, could be had with 275- or 290-horse 340s, 335-horse 383s, 375- or 390-horse 440s, or the almighty Street Hemi, which now featured hydraulic lifters for ease of maintenance. *Car Craft* magazine tested a '70 Hemicuda and it turned 13.1-second ETs. There was precious little out there that could touch 'Cudas and Challengers.

Both were real image machines and while they shared similar looks, they were in fact quite different. The Challenger's 110-inch wheelbase was 2 inches longer than that of the 'Cuda, and the two vehicles shared none of the same body panels.

Forever playing catch-up, Dodge and Plymouth introduced their ultimate ponycars—the Barracuda (left) and the Challenger (top)—in 1970. Both were available with up to 425 Hemi-produced horsepower. The rarest of the breed were the Hemi convertibles; only eight Hemicuda ragtops and nine elephant-powered Challengers were built. Both could be had with the "Shaker" fresh air hood (above).

On paper, the ultimate Mustang for 1971 was the amazing 429 Super Cobra Jet (above). But the real sleeper was the Boss 351, which had a 330-horsepower version of the 351-Cleveland engine (above right). With ram-air induction and less weight, the Boss 351 could eat the 429 for lunch. As was the case with many muscle cars, the hot Mustang engines were quickly disappearing at this time. The 428 CJ and Boss 429 were casualties in 1971.

They were tremendous cars, but in two years all the big blocks, Hemis, and multiple carbs would be gone in both the 'Cuda and the Challenger; the top power plant would be the 340 4-barrel in 1972 and 1973, and the 360 in 1974.

Fine Lines

Camaros and Firebirds for 1970 featured breath-taking new lines, although they were substantially larger than the cars they replaced. Handling was vastly improved. Engines for both were essentially carryovers, although the Z/28 got a powerful new 360-horse version of the Corvette's 350-cube LT-1 and the SS396 actually displaced 402 cubes. Rumors were running rampant that 454-powered Camaros were coming. Even the 450-horse LS6

was supposedly just around the corner, but it was almost impossible to get this car unless you lived around the corner from a place like Motion Performance in Baldwin, New York, which built its own.

Pontiac would use a little restraint in 1970 and keep the 400 as the top power plant, but for 1971 the 455 H.O. became standard in the Trans Am. It made 335 horsepower, despite a lower 8.4:1 compression, and was one of the most perfectly balanced muscle cars ever.

Both the Mustang and Cougar grew almost to midsize proportions in 1971. They were heavier, and the Cougar was now well on its way to becoming Mercury's Thunderbird. Still, there was plenty of performance left in the deck. The Boss 302 was dead, but in its place was the Boss 351 Mustang, making 330 horsepower with the help of

its canted-valve cylinder heads. The extra cubes were necessary thanks to the extra pork that came with the Mustang's new, larger shape.

While the 428 Cobra Jet was retired, as was the Boss 429, the top-rated 'Stang engines were the 429 Cobra Jet and the 429 Super Cobra Jet, which were introduced in 1970 in Ford and Mercury's intermediate-size muscle cars. They pegged the dyno at an impressive 370 and 375 hp respectively, but in reality the big-block cars were no match for the Boss 351. Tragically, neither Jet could be purchased in 1972.

Things were falling apart quickly. Although a 266-horse 351 Cobra Jet was available in 1972, it found few takers. A 275-horse 351 H.O. was also offered, but this engine made it into only about a thousand cars. Mustang performance died quietly in 1973 with the 351 Cobra Jet.

Only tiny AMC actually increased the size of its top engines in the seventies. The 343 became the 360 and the 390 the 401, but by 1971 both were hampered by lowered compression ratios. This affected all marques, not just American Motors. The 360 actually had 5 less horsepower (285) than the 343. If you ordered the 401, you got a 330-horse mill that made 430 lbs.-ft. of torque. Both were available in the Javelin or the AMX, which was no longer a two-seater but the top-of-the-line Javelin. Among the things differentiating the AMX from the Javelin were a flush-mounted screen grille, a fiberglass cowl induction hood, and slotted wheels.

To AMC's credit, it offered the 401 right to the bitter end, which came in 1974.

The last of the real muscle cars were the '73 and '74 Super Duty Firebird Trans Ams and Formulas (above and right, respectively). As street cars go, they were as quick as anything Pontiac ever produced, even in the GTO's heyday—they were capable of high 13-second quarters.

Only the Strong Survive

Sales of big-block Camaros fell off sharply after the 1970 model year; only 1,533 went out the door in 1971 and only 970 in 1972. At this point, Chevrolet would pull the plug on Rat motors. Even the solid-lifter small block bit the dust that year. For 1973 and 1974, the hottest Camaro was the Z/28 with a 245-horse L82. Pretty grim.

Pontiac was alone in its efforts to improve performance. The Trans Am and Formula could be had with the 335-horse 455 in 1971 and 1972, but the most amazing Firebirds were those ordered with the Super Duty 455. Flying in the face of rising insurance rates and Arab oil embargoes, the '73 and '74 Super Dutys were the last bastion of muscle car glory. Underrated at 310 net horsepower at 4000 rpm, they would easily pull 6000 rpm and could propel the 'Birds to low 14- and high 13-second quarter-mile ETs.

Only 43 Formulas and 252 SD Trans Ams were built in 1973. In 1974 just 57 Formulas and 943 Trans Ams were made. The T/As were equipped with shaker hood scoops that were non-

functional from the factory—the reason being California's drive-by noise standards. Many backyard tuners took the time to open up the scoops, which added another 10 to 15 horsepower.

Despite all this, Pontiac must be given a lot of credit. Though the Super Dutys lasted only two years, it continued offering 455 power through the 1976 model year. So what if the later versions were totally emasculated? What really mattered was that they were still available.

Ten Quickest Ponycars
1. 1970–1971 Hemicuda/Challenger 426
2. 1968–1970 Mustang 428 Cobra Jet/ Super Cobra Jet
3. 1967–1969 Camaro 396/375
4. 1969 Firebird Ram Air IV
5. 1969 'Cuda 440
6. 1971 Boss 351 Mustang
7. 1973–1974 Super Duty Trans Am/Formula
8. 1968 Firebird Ram Air II
9. 1968 Mercury Cougar 428 Cobra Jet
10. 1970–1971 'Cuda/Challenger 440 6-barrel.

Chapter 4

It happened on the strip
where the road
is wide
Two cool shorts standin'
side by side
Yeah, my fuel-injected
Sting Ray and a 413
We're revvin' up our
engines and it sounds
real mean...

—"Shut Down," by the Beach Boys

In 1970, the muscle car era peaked. The Corvette got its largest engine ever, the mighty 454, while the Mercury Cyclone (opposite) got its "trident" front end and the heavy 429 Cobra Jet. The ultimate executive hot rod, the 1968 Hurst/Olds (above right), sitting proudly in front of Demmer's Foundry in Lansing, Michigan, where the final assembly work was performed on these limited-edition stormers.

What would you expect from a year that saw Richard Nixon elected president? The entire nation was out of control. People were rioting in the streets, young Americans were being slaughtered in Vietnam, and men and women everywhere were protesting something.

On the lighter side, the Beatles gave us the *White Album* and the single "Hey Jude"; Denny McLain of the Detroit Tigers became the last pitcher in the major leagues to win thirty games (he actually won thirty-one); and the New York Jets won the championship of the American Football League and were just a couple of weeks from victory in Super Bowl III.

As if caught up in the same whirlpool of excitement, the Big Three offered up the most incredible lineup of muscle cars yet. It was as if the brightest minds in the industry stayed awake nights trying to come up with the ultimate combinations. Any way you look at it—styling, acceleration, handling, or panache—the 1968 supercars were amazing beyond belief.

Whether it was simply fate or just an unprecedented alignment of the stars (this was, after all, the Age of Aquarius), each of the divisions of GM, Ford, and Chrysler revamped their lineups of intermediates. That meant the GTO, Chevelle, Fairlane, Charger—every glorious offering—were all new, all outstanding.

Horsepower ratings were escalating faster than U.S. involvement in Southeast Asia, if not on paper (there were insurance companies to be concerned with), then certainly in practice. While few engines were introduced, the right pieces were already in place and top-notch hardware was being added.

There were many highlights for the class of 1968; perhaps it would be appropriate to begin with a colorful new model so interesting and so much fun that it had everybody talking.

We're referring to the Plymouth Road Runner, a bare-bones performance machine named after a Warner Bros. cartoon character. While its stylists were initially aghast at the idea of a cartoon bird adorning the flanks of their latest design (it was originally supposed to be called La Mancha), there was no denying that the concept was a stroke of marketing genius.

Dodge and Plymouth had been proving for years that you can pack every ounce of power and engineering you want into a car, but if the vehicle is not interesting, the public will stay away. The '67

The '68 Plymouth Road Runner (above) was an instant sales success thanks to its low price, potent power plants, and cartoon-character charm. The standard 383 sported all the high-performance goodies from the GTX's 440; optional was the Hemi (below left). Only New York City taxis offered an interior as spartan as that of the Road Runner (below right). Like a taxi, it had no carpeting, only rubber floor mats.

DODGE/PLYMOUTH

1968

Cu. In.	340	383	426
Bore (in.)	4.04	4.25	4.25
Stroke (in.)	3.31	3.38	3.75
Compression	10.50:1	10.00:1	10.25:1
Induction	1x4 bbl.	1x4 bbl.	2x4 bbl.
Horsepower/RPM	275/5000	335/5200	425/5000
Torque (lbs.-ft.)/RPM	340/3200	425/3400	490/4000

1968 (cont.)

Cu. In.	440
Bore (in.)	4.32
Stroke (in.)	3.75
Compression	10.10:1
Induction	1x4 bbl.
Horsepower/RPM	375/4600
Torque (lbs.-ft.)/RPM	480/3200

1969

Cu. In.	340	383
Bore (in.)	4.04	4.25
Stroke (in.)	3.31	3.38
Compression	10.50:1	10.00:1
Induction	1x4 bbl.	1x4 bbl.
Horsepower/RPM	275/5000	335/5200
Torque (lbs.-ft.)/RPM	340/3200	425/3400

1969 (cont.)

Cu. In.	440		426
Bore (in.)	4.32		4.25
Stroke (in.)	3.75		3.75
Compression	10.10:1	10.50:1	10.25:1
Induction	1x4 bbl.	3x2 bbl.	2x4 bbl.
Horsepower/RPM	375/4600	390/4700	425/5000
Torque (lbs.-ft.)/RPM	480/3200	490/3200	490/4000

1970

Cu. In.	340	383
Bore (in.)	4.04	4.25
Stroke (in.)	3.31	3.38
Compression	10.50:1	9.50:1
Induction	1x4 bbl.	1x4 bbl.
Horsepower/RPM	275/5000	335/5200
Torque (lbs.-ft.)/RPM	340/3200	425/3400

1970 (cont.)

Cu. In.	440		426
Bore (in.)	4.32		4.25
Stroke (in.)	3.75		3.75
Compression	9.70:1	10.50:1	10.25:1
Induction	1x4 bbl.	3x2 bbl.	2x4 bbl.
Horsepower/RPM	375/4600	390/4700	425/5000
Torque (lbs.-ft.)/RPM	480/3200	490/3200	490/4000

1971

Cu. In.	340	383
Bore (in.)	4.04	4.25
Stroke (in.)	3.31	3.38
Compression	10.50:1	8.50:1
Induction	1x4 bbl.	1x4 bbl.
Horsepower/RPM	275/5000	300/4800
Torque (lbs.-ft.)/RPM	340/3200	410/3400

1971 (cont.)

Cu. In.	440		426
Bore (in.)	4.32		4.25
Stroke (in.)	3.75		3.75
Compression	9.70:1	10.50:1	10.25:1
Induction	1x4 bbl.	3x2 bbl.	2x4 bbl.
Horsepower/RPM	370/4600	385/4700	425/5000
Torque (lbs.-ft.)/RPM	480/3200	490/3200	490/4000

1972

Cu. In.	340
Bore (in.)	4.04
Stroke (in.)	3.31
Compression	8.50:1
Induction	1x4 bbl.
Horsepower/RPM	240/4800
Torque (lbs.-ft.)/RPM	290/3600

1973

Cu. In.	340
Bore (in.)	4.04
Stroke (in.)	3.31
Compression	8.50:1
Induction	1x4 bbl.
Horsepower/RPM	240/4800
Torque (lbs.-ft.)/RPM	295/3600

1974

Cu. In.	360
Bore (in.)	4.00
Stroke (in.)	3.58
Compression	8.40:1
Induction	1x4 bbl.
Horsepower/RPM	245/4800
Torque (lbs.-ft.)/RPM	320/3600

Plymouth GTX and Dodge R/T were all anyone could ask for, but both cars were getting their tails kicked saleswise by the GTO and Chevelle SS. And it doesn't matter how many races you win. The bottom line is still the most important thing to any executive.

The idea for the car's name has been credited over the years to Gordon Cherry, who worked for Chrysler/Plymouth product planning manager Jim Smith. Legend has it that Cherry was struck with the brainstorm while watching Saturday morning cartoons with his children. No matter how hard he tried, Wile E. Coyote could never catch *Geococcyx Californianus*, also known as our friend the Road Runner.

There were numerous factors involved in the Road Runner's success. Foremost was that it was a 14-second supercar priced at around $3,000. The 14-second ET was achieved by supplying a hopped-up big block and bulletproof drivetrain, but leaving out all the fluff and unnecessary options.

The Road Runner succeeded admirably. For power, the indestructible 383 was fitted with the camshaft, cylinder heads, and exhaust manifolds from the mighty 440 Super Commando. This gave it an underrated 335 horsepower. The only op-

tional power plant was the Hemi. It made your choices simple.

To cut weight, "Beepers" or "Beep Beeps," as they would come to be known, came with interiors that were so spartan they could shame a New York City taxicab. Bench seats were standard; the flip-open rear windows did not roll down; and instead of carpeting, all you got was a rubber mat to cover the floor. The Road Runner was available only as a pillared coupe.

What made them so popular? As Big Brother and the Holding Company would have put it, "Cheap Thrills." Plus, there was a little bit of magic

The underrated 428 Cobra Jet (left: a '69 model) was available in any Fairlane body style, including the fastback, which was the choice for NASCAR pilots, and the lighter coupe (above).

in that bird—a Road Runner caricature on either door and another on the decklid. The horn went "Beep Beep" in the same voice as the famed cartoon character. Nor did it hurt that the new-for-'68 B-body was one of the cleanest shapes ever to come out of Motor City. It wouldn't be long before the streets of America would become flooded with Road Runners—44,598 copies that first year and 82,109 the next, darn close to smashing the GTO's sales record.

It was Everyman's muscle car.

Dodge had its own version of the Road Runner, called the Super Bee. Despite a rather cool emblem that sported a drag-racing bee (symbolic of the '68 Dodge "Scat Pack"), its reception was less favorable than that of its Plymouth cousin, a car that was its mechanical twin except for a 1-inch difference in wheelbase.

The GTX and R/T carried on with their variations of the same B-body sheet metal, but the one car that stands out above all others from the Mopar camp in 1968 is the Charger. While the look of the first-generation car was a love-it-or-hate-it proposition, the '68 was a milestone automobile. It featured recessed hideaway headlights, a Coke-bottle shape, and flying buttress roof panels with a concave backlight. It endures today as one of the benchmarks of styling.

Standard in the Charger R/T was the ferocious 440 Magnum with 375 horsepower. Naturally, the Hemi was optional. Regular Chargers could be had with anything from a Slant Six to a 383 (2- or 4-barrel). While there were some muscle cars that could run with the Charger R/T, few could match it for design or image.

First on Race Day

Ford's Total Performance program was bearing the sweet fruit of success. Even though Richard Petty won the NASCAR driving championship in a Plymouth in 1967, Ford had a very nice year with ten victories. When its redesigned intermediates hit the streets in the fall of 1967, there was no question what the stylists had in mind. The fastback version of the Fairlane 500 (and new Torino) looked like it was ready for the super speedways in showroom trim. It looked great, and its big, sloping roofline made it a natural for stock car racing. Ask David Pearson. He won the NASCAR driver's championship in a '68 Ford; in total, Fords ended up in the winner's circle twenty times.

Early on, the 390-horse 427 was the top engine available, but it was replaced later in the year by the 428 Cobra Jet, the same 335-horse screamer that made the Mustang boogie. Interiors were vastly improved as well.

Mercury was knee-deep in muscle car glory. Its Cyclone looked as good as, if not better than, its Torino counterpart. Cale Yarborough won the Daytona 500 in a Cyclone in 1968, and on the street it was also quite a hit. Mercury was delivering on its promise of winged messengers.

FORD

1968

Cu. In.	390	427	428
Bore (in.)	4.05	4.23	4.13
Stroke (in.)	3.78	3.78	3.98
Compression	10.50:1	10.90:1	10.60:1
Induction	1x4 bbl.	1x4 bbl.	1x4 bbl.
Horsepower/RPM	335/4800	390/4600	335/5200
Torque (lbs.-ft.)/RPM	427/3200	460/3200	445/3400

1969

Cu. In.	351
Bore (in.)	4.00
Stroke (in.)	3.50
Compression	10.70:1
Induction	1x4 bbl.
Horsepower/RPM	290/4800
Torque (lbs.-ft.)/RPM	385/3200

1969 (cont.)

Cu. In.	390	428
Bore (in.)	4.05	4.13
Stroke (in.)	3.78	3.98
Compression	10.50:1	10.60:1
Induction	1x4 bbl.	1x4 bbl.
Horsepower/RPM	320/4600	335/5200
Torque (lbs.-ft.)/RPM	427/3200	445/3400

1970

Cu. In.	351*
Bore (in.)	4.00
Stroke (in.)	3.50
Compression	11.00:1
Induction	1x4 bbl.
Horsepower/RPM	300/5400
Torque (lbs.-ft.)/RPM	380/3400

*Cleveland engine

1970 (cont.)

Cu. In.	428	429	429*
Bore (in.)	4.13	4.36	4.36
Stroke (in.)	3.98	3.59	3.59
Compression	10.60:1	10.50:1	11.30:1
Induction	1x4 bbl.	1x4 bbl.	1x4 bbl.
Horsepower/RPM	335/5200	360/4600	370/5400
Torque (lbs.-ft.)/RPM	445/3400	480/3400	450/3400

*Cobra Jet

1970 (cont.)

Cu. In.	429*
Bore (in.)	4.36
Stroke (in.)	3.59
Compression	11.30:1
Induction	1x4 bbl.
Horsepower/RPM	375/5600
Torque (lbs.-ft.)/RPM	450/3400

*Super Cobra Jet

1971

Cu. In.	351*
Bore (in.)	4.00
Stroke (in.)	3.50
Compression	10.70:1
Induction	1x4 bbl.
Horsepower/RPM	385/5400
Torque (lbs.-ft.)/RPM	370/3400

*Cleveland engine

1971 (cont.)

Cu. In.	429		
Bore (in.)	4.36		
Stroke (in.)	3.59		
Compression	11.30:1		
Induction	1x4 bbl.		
Horsepower/RPM	360/4600	370/5400*	375/5600**
Torque (lbs.-ft.)/RPM	480/3400	450/3400	450/3400

*Cobra Jet
**Super Cobra Jet

The 429 was available in two forms in the '71 Mustang, Cobra Jet (above) and Super Cobra Jet, which added the Drag Pack axle ratios and an oil cooler, among other things.

A-Mazing

In corporate speak, the GM intermediates were known as A-bodies. To everybody else they were just A-mazing. It was with these cars (and the new Corvette) that the General truly entered the modern era. All designs were based on a 112-inch wheelbase (3 inches shorter than the previous cars), and the new shorter, wider dimensions contributed to better ride, cornering, and all-around stability. Let's look at them in alphabetical order.

Buick GS: The stylists in Flint replaced the boxy Gran Sport of 1967 with a more shapely design that had long, sculpted sides. Power was provided by the 340-horse 400 (or 280-horse 350 if you ordered the less potent GS 350). Standard was a 3-speed manual gearbox, but a 4-speed was optional, as was a Turbo 400 automatic.

As you would expect, the interior was more posh than would be found in other GM intermediates, but also less sporting in nature.

Buick also (quietly) offered the first of its Stage packages this year. Oddly called the Stage II, it featured high-compression pistons, a special camshaft and valvetrain, and better internals. Known only to Buick engineers and hardcore racers, it was rated at 350 hp with the NHRA.

Chevrolet Chevelle SS: This car featured a bold new shape with a semi-fastback roofline, traditional Chevy quad headlights, and a more sinewy shape. The twin-domed hood was longer, the trunk shorter. (Engines mattered; luggage did not.)

The inside of the Chevelle was also redesigned. The gauges, including an unconventional (and optional) vertical bar-graph tach, were located directly in front of the driver.

For power, the SS396 had carryover power plants with 325, 350, or 375 horsepower available. Though rumors were running wild that the 427 was on its way, you could still get one only in a Corvette or a full-size Chevy from the factory.

If you preferred your muscle in a smaller package, you could now get the Chevelle's 396/375 in the compact but nose-heavy Chevy II Nova. This move was made possible by the fact that the '68 Nova was redesigned and had its engine bay widened in the process.

Top: The 1970 Stage I 455 GSX was Buick's wildest muscle car. This example turned high 13s at 100 mph in a 1992 road test. Above: The '70 LS-6 Chevelle was among the quickest muscle cars ever built, thanks to its 450-horsepower 454 mill. Even the Corvette didn't have this much power. For a real sleeper, you could get the LS-6 engine in a no-frills Chevelle (no stripes, bench seat, column shifter).

OLDSMOBILE

1968

Cu. In.	350	400	
Bore (in.)	4.06	3.87	
Stroke (in.)	3.39	4.25	
Compression	10.50:1	10.50:1	
Induction	1x4 bbl.	1x4 bbl.	
Horsepower/RPM	325/5400	350/5000*	360/5400**
Torque (lbs.-ft.)/RPM	360/3600	440/3600	440/3600

*325 hp with automatic transmission
**W-30 option

1969

Cu. In.	350	400	
Bore (in.)	4.06	3.87	
Stroke (in.)	3.39	4.25	
Compression	10.50:1	10.50:1	
Induction	1x4 bbl.	1x4 bbl.	
Horsepower/RPM	325/5400	350/5000	360/5400*
Torque (lbs.-ft.)/RPM	360/3600	440/3600	440/3600

*W-30 option

1970

Cu. In.	350	455	
Bore (in.)	4.06	4.12	
Stroke (in.)	3.39	4.25	
Compression	10.50:1	10.50:1	
Induction	1x4 bbl.	1x4 bbl.	
Horsepower/RPM	325/5400	365/5000	370/5200*
Torque (lbs.-ft.)/RPM	360/3600	500/3200	500/3600

*W-30 option

1971

Cu. In.	455	
Bore (in.)	4.12	
Stroke (in.)	4.25	
Compression	8.50:1	
Induction	1x4 bbl.	
Horsepower/RPM	340/4600	360/4700*
Torque (lbs.-ft.)/RPM	460/3200	460/3200

*W-30 option

1972

Cu. In.	350	455	
Bore (in.)	4.06	4.12	
Stroke (in.)	3.39	4.25	
Compression	8.50:1	8.50:1	
Induction	1x4 bbl.	1x4 bbl.	
Horsepower/RPM	180/4000	270/4400	300/4400*
Torque (lbs.-ft.)/RPM	275/2800	370/3200	410/3200

*W-30 option

One of the last great GM midsize performers was the '72 Olds 4-4-2 with the W-30 cold-air package. By 1973, the muscles had gone soft and the ragtop went into the history books.

Oldsmobile 4-4-2: The good folks in Lansing finally saw fit to make the 4-4-2 its own model, separate from the F-85. Styling included a nose that was reminiscent of the '67 model (quad headlights with the parking lights/turn signals mounted between the high and low beams), but in a larger, rounder shape.

Under the hood, a 400 with 350 horsepower was standard, though it was quite a bit different from the year before. While displacement remained the same, Olds changed both the bore and stroke (to 3.87 x 4.25 inches). Compression was 10.5:1. It could still be bought with the wild "Force-Air Induction" package, which gave you

13 x 2-inch scoops mounted under the bumper directing air through to the carb.

If you had the bucks, the W-30 package, with plastic inner fenders, blueprinted engine, heavy-duty rear and cooling, cold-air induction, and high-perf cam, was also available. It was rated at 360 horsepower.

Oldsmobile also offered a "junior supercar" in 1968. The Ram Rod W-31 was a 325-horse 350 optional for $205 in the Cutlass only. It had a 3.91 rear standard, small-port 350 heads with larger intake valves, and a long-duration camshaft. It could wind to 6000 rpm and was a true bargain-basement performer.

PONTIAC

1968

Cu. In.	350	400	
Bore (in.)	3.88	4.12	
Stroke (in.)	3.75	3.75	
Compression	10.50:1	10.75:1	
Induction	1x4 bbl.	1x4 bbl.	
Horsepower/RPM	320/5100	350/5000	360/5100*
Torque (lbs.-ft.)/RPM	380/3200	445/3000	445/3600

*H.O.

1968 (cont.)

Cu. In.	400
Bore (in.)	4.12
Stroke (in.)	3.75
Compression	10.75:1
Induction	1x4 bbl.
Horsepower/RPM	360/5400
Torque (lbs.-ft.)/RPM	445/3800*

*Ram Air II

1969

Cu. In.	350	400	
Bore (in.)	3.88	4.12	
Stroke (in.)	3.75	3.75	
Compression	10.50:1	10.75:1	
Induction	1x4 bbl.	1x4 bbl.	
Horsepower/RPM	325/5100	350/5000	366/5100*
Torque (lbs.-ft.)/RPM	380/3200	450/3000	445/3600

*Ram Air III

1969 (cont.)

Cu. In.	400
Bore (in.)	4.12
Stroke (in.)	3.75
Compression	10.75:1
Induction	1x4 bbl.
Horsepower/RPM	370/5500
Torque (lbs.-ft.)/RPM	445/3900*

*Ram Air IV

1970

Cu. In.	400		
Bore (in.)	4.12		
Stroke (in.)	3.75		
Compression	10.00:1	10.25:1	10.50:1
Induction	1x4 bbl.	1x4 bbl.	1x4 bbl.
Horsepower/RPM	330/4800*	350/5000	366/5100**
Torque (lbs.-ft.)/RPM	445/2900	445/3000	445/3600

*Tempest only, automatic transmission only
**Ram Air III

1970 (cont.)

Cu. In.	400	455
Bore (in.)	4.12	4.15
Stroke (in.)	3.75	4.21
Compression	10.50:1	10.25:1
Induction	1x4 bbl.	1x4 bbl.
Horsepower/RPM	370/5500	360/4300
Torque (lbs.-ft.)/RPM	445/3900*	500/2700

*Ram Air IV

1971

Cu. In.	400	455	
Bore (in.)	4.12	4.15	
Stroke (in.)	3.75	4.21	
Compression	8.20:1	8.20:1	8.40:1
Induction	1x4 bbl.	1x4 bbl.	1x4 bbl.
Horsepower/RPM	300/5000	325/4400	335/4800*
Torque (lbs.-ft.)/RPM	430/3400	455/3200	480/3600

*455 H.O.

1972

Cu. In.	400	455	
Bore (in.)	4.12	4.15	
Stroke (in.)	3.75	4.21	
Compression	8.20:1	8.20:1	8.40:1
Induction	1x4 bbl.	1x4 bbl.	1x4 bbl.
Horsepower/RPM	250/4400	250/3600	300/4000*
Torque (lbs.-ft.)/RPM	325/3200	475/3400	415/3200

*455 H.O.

1973

Cu. In.	400	455
Bore (in.)	4.12	4.15
Stroke (in.)	3.75	4.21
Compression	8.00:1	8.20:1
Induction	1x4 bbl.	1x4 bbl.
Horsepower/RPM	230/4400	250/4000
Torque (lbs.-ft.)/RPM	325/3200	370/2800

1974

Cu. In.	350
Bore (in.)	3.88
Stroke (in.)	3.75
Compression	7.60:1
Induction	1x4 bbl.
Horsepower/RPM	200/4400
Torque (lbs.-ft.)/RPM	295/2800

Pontiac GTO: Among the '68 GTO's innovations was the Endura front bumper. Made of high-density urethane foam, it was painted to match the color of the car and blend in with the rest of the bodywork, giving the car a "bumperless" appearance.

Because GM styling chief Bill Mitchell was afraid it might detract from sales, you could order a GTO with a Tempest/LeMans chrome bumper early in the model year. He was off the mark. The Endura nose created a sensation. Not only did it look outstanding, but it was resistant to damage from minor impacts. Television commercials featured an actor whacking a bumper with a sledgehammer to demonstrate its toughness. Hideaway headlights were a popular option with the Endura bumper—the two seemed made for each other.

Pontiac upped the standard motor's rating to 350 horsepower (although it contained no changes), and two other 400-cubic-inch V8s were for the taking. Both were rated at 360 horsepower, the former called the 400 H.O., the latter (and much more powerful) the Ram Air II with free-breathing round-port cylinder heads (which were a midyear introduction).

Magazines were able to get the Ram Air Goats to turn easy mid- to high 14-second quarter-mile times, and almost everyone raved about their superior interior and handling. Muscle car customers responded enthusiastically, snapping up 87,684 vehicles. The success of the '68 GTO helped Pontiac Motor Division sell more than 900,000 units for the first time. It seemed that DeLorean and company could do no wrong. And they still had one more trick up their sleeve.

Opposite: With its Coke-bottle styling, super-clean Enduro front bumper, and hideaway headlights, the '69 GTO (top) was a road-going dream machine. While the original plans for the 1969 GTO Judge called for it to be a Road Runner–style, bare-bones supercar, it ended up being a top-of-the-line model. The earliest versions were painted Carousel Red (bottom), while later editions could be had in a variety of colors. The Arab oil embargo, ultra-high insurance rates, and tightening emissions standards would conspire to kill off most muscle cars in less than four years.

"The Judge Can Be Bought"

So said Pontiac's advertising when the new-for-'69 GTO Judge hit the showrooms. Initially, this vehicle was supposed to be Pontiac's budget-priced answer to the Plymouth Road Runner. By the time everyone got his two cents' worth in, the Judge was actually more festooned with options and geegaws than previous top-of-the-line Tigers. Most noticeable were its brightly colored side stripes, tacky rear spoiler, and optional hood-mounted tach. Its name, in big, bold letters on the side, was taken from a skit from TV's popular comedy show *Laugh-In* (as in "Heah come da judge...").

Unlike regular GTOs, which had the 350-horse 400 as standard equipment, the Judge packed the 366-horse Ram Air III 400 as its base mill. If you had a little extra spending money, you could be first on your block with the stout 370-horse Ram Air IV, a new motor based on the 1968 RA II but with re-designed round port heads, a 308/320-degree cam, high-lift rocker arms, and, of course, a functional cold-air hood.

When it was first introduced, many people considered the Judge a goof, a joke of a muscle car. The GTO had gotten heavier and more loaded with power-robbing options, and the first 5,000 Judges built were Carousel Red (a nice way of saying

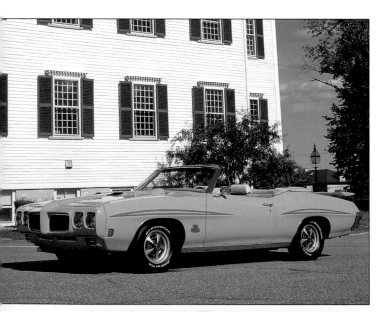

The Great One by Pontiac.

Above: Take a good look at this GTO ad (right). Chances are you have never seen it before. Detriot's Woodward Avenue was one of the most notorious street-racing venues in the United States, and this fact was not lost on GM's high-ranking executives, who indeed "knew the rest of the story." They ordered the ad pulled after it ran only once, in the December 1967 issue of *Motor Trend* magazine. The 1970 GTO (left) gained notoriety of its own after one co-starred in the cult street-racing film *Two-Lane Blacktop*, which starred drummer Dennis Wilson of the Beach Boys and singer James Taylor.

You know the rest of the story.

orange). Studies showed that the rear spoiler actually hindered, rather than helped, aerodynamics. This matters little today. The Judges were considered fairly strong runners and now rank among the most sought-after muscle cars by collectors.

While the GTO received only a moderate face-lift, the 4-4-2 was in for some big changes. The basic body shape was about the same, but the nose and taillights were completely redesigned.

Under the hood, things remained the same, with the 350-hp 400 standard and 360 with Force-Air Induction optional. What about the W-30? It, too, was pretty much a repeat from 1968. While its inherent virtue made it a favorite of Olds loyalists, this was a time of more! More! MORE! What could Lansing do to bolster its image?

The answer came in the form of Dr. Oldsmobile, a kind of psychedelic Dr. Frankenstein character who, with his W-machines, terrorized street and strip alike. It was one of the more memorable ad campaigns of the supercar era. As it had in 1968, Olds turned once again to Hurst Performance to build a limited-edition, 455-powered "executive hot rod." Though down 10 horsepower from 1968 (380 vs. 390), the Hurst/Olds was a potent performer. The strong W-31 Cutlass was still available, too.

Chevrolet's hot-selling Chevelle SS396 could be had with up to 375 horsepower, but that really wasn't enough anymore. Chevy freaks would have been happy with any one of the six versions of the 427 that was propelling the Corvette to obscene quarter-mile times, but such wasn't to be.

Some lucky stiffs were able to pick up COPO Chevelles. COPO stood for Central Office Production Order, and while it technically shouldn't have been able to happen, certain dealers—among them Yenko, Berger, and Nickey Chevrolet—were able to obtain legitimate factory 427/425 horse Chevelles (and Camaros, too). They weren't cheap, but if you had the dough, they provided as much go as you were likely to need.

In 1969 Buick was able to improve on its GS400. This vehicle received a hood that could be made functional, its styling was more refined, and the Stage I package was introduced.

Consisting of a reworked Quadrajet 4-barrel (so the secondaries opened quicker), a high-lift cam, larger-diameter (2¼-inch) exhaust pipes, a

CHEVROLET

1968

Cu. In.	327	
Bore (in.)	4.00	
Stroke (in.)	3.25	
Compression	10.00:1	11.00:1
Induction	1x4 bbl.	1x4 bbl.
Horsepower/RPM	300/5000	350/5800
Torque (lbs.-ft.)/RPM	360/3400	360/3600

1968 (cont.)

Cu. In.	396		
Bore (in.)	4.094		
Stroke (in.)	3.76		
Compression	10.25:1		11.00:1
Induction	1x4 bbl.		1x4 bbl.
Horsepower/RPM	325/4800	350/5200	375/5600
Torque (lbs.-ft.)/RPM	410/3200	415/3400	415/3600

1968 (cont.)

Cu. In.	427		
Bore (in.)	4.25		
Stroke (in.)	3.76		
Compression	10.25:1		
Induction	1x4 bbl.		3x2 bbl.
Horsepower/RPM	385/5200	390/5400	400/5400
Torque (lbs.-ft.)/RPM	460/3400	460/3600	460/3600

1968 (cont.)

Cu. In.	427*	
Bore (in.)	4.25	
Stroke (in.)	3.76	
Compression	12.50:1	11.00:1
Induction	1x4 bbl.	3x2 bbl.
Horsepower/RPM	430/5200	435/5800
Torque (lbs.-ft.)/RPM	450/4400	460/4000
*L-88		

1969

Cu. In.	350	
Bore (in.)	4.00	
Stroke (in.)	3.48	
Compression	10.25:1	11.00:1
Induction	1x4 bbl.	1x4 bbl.
Horsepower/RPM	300/4800	350/5600
Torque (lbs.-ft.)/RPM	380/3200	380/3600

1969 (cont.)

Cu. In.	396		
Bore (in.)	4.094		
Stroke (in.)	3.76		
Compression	10.25:1		11.00:1
Induction	1x4 bbl.		1x4 bbl.
Horsepower/RPM	325/4800	350/5200	375/5600
Torque (lbs.-ft.)/RPM	410/3200	415/3400	415/3600

1969 (cont.)

Cu. In.	427		
Bore (in.)	4.25		
Stroke (in.)	3.76		
Compression	10.25:1		
Induction	1x4 bbl.		3x2 bbl.
Horsepower/RPM	335/4800	390/5400	400/5400
Torque (lbs.-ft.)/RPM	470/3200	460/3600	460/3600

1969 (cont.)

Cu. In.	427*		
Bore (in.)	4.25		
Stroke (in.)	3.76		
Compression	12.50:1	11.00:1	11.00:1
Induction	1x4 bbl.	3x2 bbl.	1x4 bbl.
Horsepower/RPM	430/5200	435/5800	425/5600
Torque (lbs.-ft.)/RPM	450/4400	460/4000	460/4000
*L-88			

1970

Cu. In.	350		
Bore (in.)	4.00		
Stroke (in.)	3.48		
Compression	10.25:1	11.00:1	
Induction	1x4 bbl.	1x4 bbl.	
Horsepower/RPM	300/4800	350/5600	370/6000
Torque (lbs.-ft.)/RPM	380/3200	380/3600	380/4000

1970 (cont.)

Cu. In.	402	
Bore (in.)	4.126	
Stroke (in.)	3.76	
Compression	10.25:1	11.00:1
Induction	1x4 bbl.	1x4 bbl.
Horsepower/RPM	350/4800	375/5600
Torque (lbs.-ft.)/RPM	415/3400	415/3600

1970 (cont.)

Cu. In.	454		
Bore (in.)	4.25		
Stroke (in.)	4.00		
Compression	10.25:1		11.25:1
Induction	1x4 bbl.		1x4 bbl.
Horsepower/RPM	360/4400	390/4800	450/5600
Torque (lbs.-ft.)/RPM	500/3200	500/3400	500/3600

1971

Cu. In.	350
Bore (in.)	4.00
Stroke (in.)	3.48
Compression	9:00:1
Induction	1x4 bbl.
Horsepower/RPM	330/5600
Torque (lbs.-ft.)/RPM	360/4000

1971 (cont.)

Cu. In.	402
Bore (in.)	4.126
Stroke (in.)	3.76
Compression	8.50:1
Induction	1x4 bbl.
Horsepower/RPM	300/4800
Torque (lbs.-ft.)/RPM	400/3200

1971 (cont.)

Cu. In.	454	
Bore (in.)	4.25	
Stroke (in.)	4.00	
Compression	8.50:1	9.00:1
Induction	1x4 bbl.	1x4 bbl.
Horsepower/RPM	365/4800	425/5600
Torque (lbs.-ft.)/RPM	465/3200	475/4000

1972

Cu. In.	350
Bore (in.)	4.00
Stroke (in.)	3.48
Compression	9:00:1
Induction	1x4 bbl.
Horsepower/RPM	255/5600
Torque (lbs.-ft.)/RPM	280/4000

1972 (cont.)

Cu. In.	402
Bore (in.)	4.126
Stroke (in.)	3.76
Compression	8.50:1
Induction	1x4 bbl.
Horsepower/RPM	240/4400
Torque (lbs.-ft.)/RPM	345/3200

1972 (cont.)

Cu. In.	454
Bore (in.)	4.25
Stroke (in.)	4.00
Compression	8.50:1
Induction	1x4 bbl.
Horsepower/RPM	270/4400
Torque (lbs.-ft.)/RPM	390/3200

functional cold-air hood, and a 3.64 Positraction rear (3.42 if you ordered A/C), the Stage I produced a brawny 350 horsepower at 5000 revs. Only 1,256 were built and the package received little in the way of press. I was able to test one, and found it stopped the clocks at an impressive 14.74 at almost 93 mph despite weighing in at over two tons. No one can ever say Buicks don't make torque! And Stage I versions had 440 lbs.-ft. of it. Sixty mph came up in 6.6 seconds.

The base GS400 was no slug, either, thanks to 340 horsepower. And the Stage II was still out there if you had a serious racing habit.

A Six-Pack to (Really) Go

Because the hardtop Road Runner (introduced in late 1968) was so successful, Plymouth decided to offer it in a convertible body as well.

But these cars were really of little consequence. For street freaks and drag racers alike, the ultimate

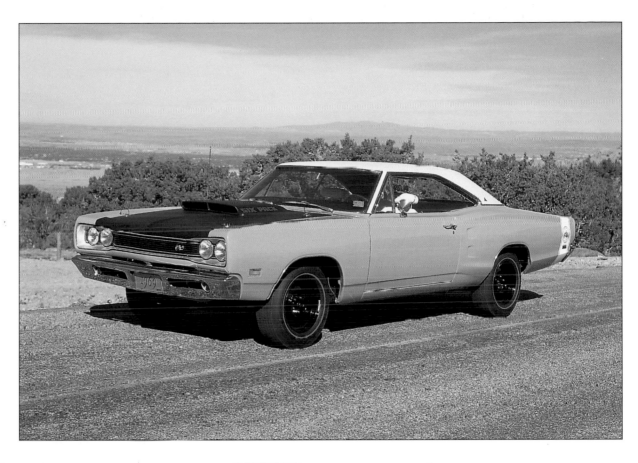

expressions of muscle car madness were the '69½ 440 Six-Barrel (Six-Pack if you got the Dodge) Road Runner and Super Bee.

These vehicles were little more than purpose-built street racers. Each had a fiberglass lift-off hood with a molded-in scoop big enough to swallow a Volkswagen. To save weight, no hinges were used; the hood was held down by four NASCAR-style hood pins. Remove the unique bonnet and you would discover 440 cubic inches of pain and devastation. A special camshaft, valves, springs, and rockers were standard, and so was the drag-oriented 4.10 Sure-Grip Dana rear. But it was the induction system, a trio of Holley 2-barrel carbs on an aluminum Chrysler/Edelbrock intake manifold, that made it a vehicle to be feared.

What you didn't get was a lot of fluff. Black-painted wheels with chrome lug nuts and beefy G70x15 Polyglas tires were the only rolling stock available. With 390 horsepower and 490 lbs.-ft. of torque, Plymouth boasted that the Six-Barrel would turn a 13-second flat ET at over 111 mph.

Chrysler's stylists did a terrific job of fine-tuning the B-bodies, especially the Charger, which received a split bumper grille and horizontal taillights

Top: Few muscle cars came as well equipped for street-racing duty as the '69½ 440 Six Pack Dodge Super Bee (and its cousin, the 440 Six-Bbl. Plymouth Road Runner). Both used heavy-duty suspensions, fiberglass lift-off hoods, and three Holley 2-barrel carbs on an Edelbrock intake manifold. The black wheels with chrome lug nuts were standard. Above: The standard '69 Super Bee was nothing to be scoffed at either, thanks to its 383 engine that featured the best parts from the 375-horsepower 440 mill from the R/T.

that made it look even tougher from behind than it had before.

Actually, super-speedway results from 1968 showed that the shapely Charger body wasn't nearly as aerodynamic as engineers had hoped. Because of this, two new models—the Charger 500 and the Charger Daytona—were introduced solely to qualify for NASCAR. The 500 had a flush grille (with exposed headlights) and flush backlight for better airflow. The Daytona had an enormous 2-foot-tall wing on the rear deck and an extended sloping nose. When Chrysler Corp. wouldn't let Richard Petty switch from Plymouth to Dodge for one of these rides, he jumped ship entirely to Ford. To racing fans, it was like the Red Sox trading Babe Ruth to the Yankees.

The car that stole Petty away was the Torino Talladega, another slope-nosed machine. While you wouldn't call this car pretty, it did work. Petty won ten races in 1968 (his only year with Ford). David Pearson, driving the Holman & Moody Talladega, won the crown. The following year, Plymouth lured the King back with a variation of the Daytona based on the Road Runner, aptly dubbed the Superbird.

For Ford's intermediates, 1969 was pretty much a carryover year. While the Talladega and Cyclone Spoiler II cousin were built to legalize them for Bill France and friends (NASCAR), it was more a year of enjoying the fruits of 1968's hard labor. All the screaming small blocks were either gone or, in the case of the Mustang's Boss 302, not available. The 428 Cobra Jet was enjoying tremendous success, both in sales and in competition.

Shaped by the Wind

In the sixties, Ford product planners worked on a two-year cycle. That meant that 1970 would see the introduction of another all-new intermediate. And in keeping with Ford's annoying habit of continually introducing completely new engine families, the 429 replaced the tremendous 428 in the Torino and Cyclone, with varying degrees of success.

From a styling standpoint, the new bodies were attractive and modern. Both were available as coupes, and the Torino line offered a "SportsRoof" fastback as well. Ford advertising said the SportsRoof was "shaped by the wind." Ford also had high hopes for the Torino Fastback in NASCAR competition.

Unfortunately, it seemed that the wind they spoke of was an ill one. The new Torinos were actually slower and less stable on the highbanks than the cars they replaced. This forced many drivers to revert to their old Talladegas.

Aerodynamics count for little on the street, though, and here is where the sleek SportsRoof design was a hit. You could get the new 300-horse 351 Cleveland, either with or without a Ram Air shaker hood. Next up on the option sheet was the 360 horse Torino Cobra backed by a tough Top Loader 4-speed and heavy-duty suspension.

This was small-time compared to the 429 Cobra Jet and Super Cobra Jet options. The regular CJ gave you 11.3:1 compression, a 2-bolt main block, and a 700 cfm carburetor—good for 370 hp at 5400 rpm. If you went for the SCJ, you were very likely a hardcore gearhead. As with the 428 Super Cobra Jet, you got it by checking off the Drag Pack option on the order sheet. Along with the 3.91 or 4.30 gears, you received (among other things) a 375-horsepower engine with 11.5:1 compression, a 4-bolt main block, a solid-lifter cam, free-breathing heads, cast-iron headers, and a 780 cfm Holley carb.

Cars so equipped were plenty potent, and they had to be—1970 was the year General Motors finally took off its gloves and entered the ring as a bare-knuckled brawler. Maybe it was because it knew it would be lowering compression ratios in 1971 and detuning its most potent power plants. Or maybe it was because it was tired of the mega-inch Mopars and Fords getting a lion's share of the good press. Whatever its reasoning, 1970 was the year GM allowed its divisions to install engines of more than 400 cubic inches in its intermediate supercars.

Suddenly, the streets were alive with the sound of 454 Chevelles, 455 GTOs, 4-4-2s, and Gran

By 1970, image was becoming as important as performance. This '70 Torino GT is a good example with its hideaway headlights, bright color, and "strobe" tape stripes, which changed colors as light hit them.

With 510 lbs.-ft. of torque from its 1970 Stage I 455, Buick's GSX was a bolt out of the blue from a company considered to be a purveyor of doctor's cars. For 1970, the GSX came in Saturn Yellow or Apollo White.

Sports, engines shrieking with power as they strained to reach their redlines—and beyond. The top versions of each of these power plants were thinly disguised race motors.

Performancewise, you would have to put the LS-6 Chevelle and Stage I 455 Buick ahead of the W-30 4-4-2 and 455 Goat. The LS-6 was rated at an incredible 450 horsepower, 90 more than the 455 Buick. But the Buick was way underrated. This engine carried 510 lbs.-ft. of torque—enough to knock the earth off its axis, never mind launch a two-ton Buick. When wrapped in the striped and spoilered GSX, which was Flint's answer to the Judge, you had one of the most nefarious automobiles imaginable.

Still, the mainstays were the SS396 (which now actually displaced 402 cubic inches, but Chevy had spent too much time and money building up the 396's image to change the name) and the Buick GS455.

Pontiac's 455 was a bored and stroked version of its 428. Surprisingly, not much power was wrung out of it. It made only 10 more horsepower than the standard 350-horse 400, 6 less than the optional Ram Air III, and 10 fewer than the Ram Air IV. It was more an image-maker than a performance automobile. Certainly, if Chevy, Buick, and Olds were zooming past the 450-cube mark, Pontiac had to do so as well. The reality was that the 455 was a good, torquey engine—the perfect power plant if you wanted to load your Goat with every conceivable option. More serious Poncho enthusiasts chose the Ram Air III and IV.

Often overlooked because of their scarcity, the fastest midsize Pontiacs in 1970 might have been the Tempest T-37 and GT-37. These were low-line pillared hardtops, which made them much lighter than the ever porkier GTO, but they were available with the 330-horse 400 with an automatic and the 366-horse Ram Air III engine, except without the

BUICK

1968

Cu. In.	350	400
Bore (in.)	3.80	4.04
Stroke (in.)	3.85	3.90
Compression	10.25:1	10.25:1
Induction	1x4 bbl.	1x4 bbl.
Horsepower/RPM	280/4600	340/5000
Torque (lbs.-ft.)/RPM	375/2800	440/3200

1969

Cu. In.	350	400	400*
Bore (in.)	3.80	4.04	4.04
Stroke (in.)	3.85	3.90	3.90
Compression	10.25:1	10.25:1	10.25:1
Induction	1x4 bbl.	1x4 bbl.	1x4 bbl.
Horsepower/RPM	280/4600	340/5000	350/5000
Torque (lbs.-ft.)/RPM	375/2800	440/3200	440/3200

*Stage 1

1970

Cu. In.	350	455	455*
Bore (in.)	3.80	4.31	4.31
Stroke (in.)	3.85	3.90	3.90
Compression	10.25:1	10.00:1	10.50:1
Induction	1x4 bbl.	1x4 bbl.	1x4 bbl.
Horsepower/RPM	285/4600	350/4600	360/4600
Torque (lbs.-ft.)/RPM	375/3200	510/2600	510/2600

*Stage 1

1971

Cu. In.	350	455	455*
Bore (in.)	3.80	4.31	4.31
Stroke (in.)	3.85	3.90	3.90
Compression	8.50:1	8.50:1	8.50:1
Induction	1x4 bbl.	1x4 bbl.	1x4 bbl.
Horsepower/RPM	260/4600	315/4600	345/5000
Torque (lbs.-ft.)/RPM	360/3200	450/2600	460/3000

*Stage 1

1972

Cu. In.	455	455*
Bore (in.)	4.31	4.31
Stroke (in.)	3.90	3.90
Compression	10.00:1	10.50:1
Induction	1x4 bbl.	1x4 bbl.
Horsepower/RPM	260/4400	270/4400
Torque (lbs.-ft.)/RPM	380/2800	390/3000

*Stage 1

Ram Air hardware, if you took the 4-speed. For 1971 they were even wilder, thanks to a healthy dose of available 455 H.O. with 335 horsepower (available only with the 4-speed).

Dr. Oldsmobile's latest creation was definitely built for go. The W-30 455 made 370 honest horsepower and 500 lbs.-ft. of torque, and came standard with a fiberglass ram-air hood (optional on lesser 4-4-2s), plastic inner fenders, an aluminum intake manifold, and a host of other goodies. Performance options were plentiful, including gear ratios up to 4.33:1, an aluminum center section for the rear end (W-27), and a Hurst Dual Gate shifter if you had the automatic.

"Announcing a New Kind of Runner"

For 1970 neither Plymouth nor Dodge offered much that was new. The Hemi got hydraulic lifters for ease of maintenance and the high-performance 440s got a slightly lower compression ratio. Stylists improved the Road Runner, GTX, and 'Cuda, but slightly spoiled the R/T, Super Bee, and Charger. There wasn't need to change much; they were playing poker and they held the aces.

Actually, the most interesting nonponycar to come out of Plymouth in 1970 was its new Superbird. Mopars have always been popular in the deep South, and NASCAR, which trailed only Jesus Christ and George Wallace in popularity down there, was just a few years removed from its moonshine-running roots.

To capitalize on all this, and to promote the winged warrior and trumpet its stock car racing success, Plymouth's ad agency placed a Superbird in front of a tobacco road shack, complete with still, and surrounded it with what can only be described as the inbred cousins of the Beverly Hillbillies. It proclaimed, "Announcing A New Kind Of Runner."

"Down in Thunder Road country, in the land of the goodolboy and goodolcar, they speak longingly of the goodoldays and ol' Curtis and ol' Junior and the ol' J-hook and so on.

"Some folks would even have you believe the era is still alive..."

One look at this photo and there's no doubting Mopar's commitment to performance in 1970. From front to rear, we have a Dodge Challenger T/A, a Plymouth Hemicuda, a Road Runner, and a Superbird. The T/A was designed to compete in SCCA Trans-Am racing, the 'Cuda and the Road Runner in drag racing, and the Superbird in NASCAR competition.

Muscle Car Road Tests: Fact or Fiction?

Get any group of muscle car enthusiasts together and the conversation will eventually turn to which cars were the fastest. The well-read among them will start spouting off elapsed time numbers and mile per hour figures from magazines as if these facts were gospel.

The reality is that some of these reported test figures have little to do with how a car is actually capable of performing. One reason that old road tests are unreliable is varying natural conditions. A 389 GTO tested at a sea-level track with a competent driver will easily run a second faster than one tested at a high-altitude track with a driver of marginal skill. Was the temperature one hundred degrees or fifty-five? The former would kill ETs, the latter enhance them.

Another important factor is the kind of timing equipment used. Some magazines relied on drag-strip timing equipment; others used very accurate fifth wheels; some used stopwatches or simply invented results that suited their needs.

Car Life usually made performance evaluations with full gas tanks and two people in the car. While this is a good indicator of how a car would do in the stoplight grand prix on cruise night, it only hints at the full potential.

Driving style also enters the picture—to powershift or not to powershift? But certainly, the biggest variable was whether or not the vehicle tested was stock. Automobile companies knew that sales were directly linked to ETs published in the automotive press. Pontiac's shenanigans were discussed earlier, but everyone was guilty to one degree or another. Ford test cars would routinely show up in Holman & Moody trailers.

On the other hand, many stock muscle cars could run much faster than was reported by magazines. The majority of journalists are writers first and race drivers second—on a good day. This is one of the reasons test cars were juiced in the first place. The Big Three couldn't risk their hot new model going too slow in print because the driver wasn't sure which end of it to point down the track.

It certainly was an amazing era, and it was coming to a halt faster than anyone realized at the time. Intense pressure from the safety lobby and insurance companies, plus tightening emissions regulations and unleaded fuel, were going to drive the great American muscle cars out of existence. The funeral was less than five years away.

This Is the End

The downward spiral began in 1971 when General Motors took the first big step by lowering compression ratios and detuning all its supercars in preparation for the imminent arrival of unleaded fuel. Immediately, power dropped noticeably. And new emissions control devices siphoned away even more grunt.

All the titans of the previous year were being emasculated. Only the Corvette, bless its fiberglass heart, held on. While the ground-pounding big blocks were disappearing quickly, the LS-6 soldiered on with 425 horsepower in the mighty Sting Ray. While compression dropped, it received aluminum cylinder heads. Even with economy 3.36 gearing and stock street tires, *Car Craft* got one to go 13.72 at 102 mph.

One of the few shining stars of the early 1970s was the '71 455 H.O. Pontiac. Its use in the Formula and Trans Am was discussed in chapter 3, but it warrants a second notice. Here was a low-compression mill that had stump-pulling torque, decent horsepower, and the easygoing temperament Poncho motors were famous for.

And while Ford and Chrysler held the line on compression for one last year, many of the street legends disappeared. Not making the call to 1971 was the Chrysler 340 6-barrel. The Boss 429, Boss 302, and 428 Cobra Jet Fords all slipped into history, to be followed a year later by the 429 Cobra Jet.

Still, the mondo 440 6-barrel survived and thrived in the fresh B-body sheet metal of the Road Runner, GTX, and Charger (the Super Bee now be-

Almost never seen today (and rarely seen in the sixties for that matter) was the '69 Cyclone Spoiler. This one has the Cale Yarborough Special graphics, which included red and white paint. The Dan Gurney model came in blue and white.

came an option on this car). Hanging on for one last battle was the Street Hemi, though it would head for the big boneyard in the sky at the end of the model year. It was a sad time. The 440 with three deuces would somehow play through 1972, the same year the 383 was replaced by the 255-horse 400.

By 1973, performance was a four-letter word around Detroit. The Road Runner continued with the 400 (it was called the Road Runner GTX if you ordered the 440), but the Charger was being prepped for life as a personal luxury car. If you wanted to go fast in a Mopar, you ordered a 340 (or a 360 in 1974) Duster or Dart. While not the giant-killers they were in the late sixties, they offered decent power in a relatively light package. They were as quick as anything else out there, including the Corvette.

But what about the car that started it all? GTO styling was based on the new-for-'73 GM Colonnade body, and while this is always a subjective area, the Pontiac version was a fairly homely vehicle. Sales fell to 4,806. Had the GTO gotten the Super Duty 455 as it was supposed to, it wouldn't have been so grim. Instead, the 250-horse 455 was the only optional mill. Standard was a 230-horse 400.

For 1974 Pontiac based the GTO on the Ventura—that division's version of the compact Chevy Nova. Only the 350 4-barrel was available, albeit with a real shaker hood scoop and dual exhaust. While sales were better than in 1973 (7,058), it was a dreadful excuse for a performance car. Pontiac mercifully held the funeral soon thereafter.

Ten Quickest Muscle Cars, 1968–1974

1. 1968–1969 Corvette 427/435 hp
2. 1968–1971 Dodge/Plymouth Hemi
3. 1970 Buick GS Stage I 455
4. 1969½ Road Runner/Super Bee 440-6V
5. 1970 Chevelle SS454 LS-6
6. 1971 Corvette LS-6
7. 1970 Corvette LT-1 350/370 hp
8. 1968 Hurst/Olds 455/390 hp
9. 1969 Pontiac GTO Ram Air IV
10. 1970 Oldsmobile 4-4-2 W-30

The last year for a big-block Challenger (above) was 1971. It was the last hurrah for the 383, both 440s (4-barrel and Six-Pack), and the Street Hemi in Dodge's ponycar. While the Challenger was awesome, it didn't pack enough oats to catch the '69 427 Corvette (top).

Chapter 5

*I took my Cobra down
to the track
Hitched to the back of
my Cadillac
Everyone was there, just
waitin' for me
There were plenty of
Sting Rays and
XKEs...*

—"Hey Little Cobra,"
by the Rip Chords

The last of the "real" Shelby Mustangs was the '67 (opposite). Available for the first time with either a 289 or a dual quad 428, the '67 was the last of the breed to focus more on performance than luxury. When set up for racing, the '65 GT350s (above right) often used the optional fiberglass lower valance for improved cooling.

Even at the height of the muscle car era, there were certain cars that the Big Three and little American Motors couldn't build—for political, financial, or marketing reasons. This created fabulous opportunities for men like Carroll Shelby, George Hurst, and Don Yenko, each of whom possessed inordinate amounts of intelligence, engineering brilliance, and marketing savvy. They stood ready to profit and, in the process, churn out some of history's most remarkable—and in many cases, insane—automobiles.

Several factors were at work. By corporate edict, none of General Motors' divisions could produce intermediate or smaller cars with engine capacity greater than 400 cubic inches. This left them vulnerable since neither Ford nor Chrysler had such a policy. American Motors, perpetually strapped for money, needed to cash in on the supercar market, but it could not divert funds from its bread-and-butter product.

Ford realized early on that it made sense to play off the success of Shelby's Cobra program. It gave the Fairlanes and Mustangs—in fact, the whole line—image and the kind of technology and parts that might be considered too expensive or too uncompromising in a mass-produced vehicle.

Hurst's Image Machines

American Motors got little respect during the early muscle car years, primarily because it offered nothing in the way of a high-performance automobile until the release of the AMX and Javelin. A handful of 343 V8–powered Rogues were built in 1968, but they had no impact on either street or strip. This created quite a dilemma for the struggling company from Kenosha, Wisconsin. The entire car-buying public had gone performance-mad, and American Motors had precious little to offer consumers.

That changed in 1969. By teaming up with Hurst Performance (of shifter fame), AMC was able to unleash a surprisingly fast pocket rocket. Dubbed the Hurst SC/Rambler, it was a compact car powered by AMC's largest engine: the 315-horse 390 from the AMX. While it may have given up some horsepower, it weighed in at barely 3,000 pounds. This gave it commendable performance;

Road Test magazine clocked one at 14.14 at 100.44 mph in the quarter-mile.

Like each of its muscle car brothers, there was more to the SC/Rambler than sheer acceleration. Its Borg-Warner 4-speed transmission had a Hurst shifter, and a 3.54:1 Twin Grip rear and functional ram-air hood came standard. While it was fairly sedate on the inside (gray vinyl seats with red, white, and blue headrests and a Sun tach on the steering column), its paint schemes were another story.

Initially, a run of five hundred cars was planned. All were white with red sides and blue stripes running the length of the vehicle. The upward-tilting hood scoop had the word "AIR" written on top, and the engine's displacement was spelled out in big, bold numbers right in front of the scoop. The wheels were AMC's five-spoke design painted the same blue as the stripes. This was known as the "A" paint scheme.

Because the first five hundred copies of the SC/Rambler were snapped up so fast, a second

run was ordered. These had substantially toned-down paint (the "B" scheme), although they were hardly what you would call subtle. Only 1,512 were built.

That same year, Hurst was called upon to help out on a number of AMX Super/Stock drag cars. In keeping with AMC's patriotic image, some left the factory in red, white, and blue paint jobs, although others were plain white. Fifty-four of them were built and all had dash plaques with their serial numbers on them (they were built sequentially from 12,567 to 12,620).

All came with special 390s with 340 horsepower. Helping boost their output were dual Holley 650s on an aluminum Edelbrock cross-ram intake. The cylinder heads were specially prepped by Crane Cams and compression was a very un-AMC-like 12.3:1. Carrying away the fumes was a set of Doug Thorley headers.

A 4.44:1 Twin Grip was standard, as was a set of traction bars. Being race cars, they were

Thanks to their advantageous power-to-weight ratios, Hurst SC/Ramblers are still making noise at drag strips today. This one sports non-stock tow bars on the front bumper and light-weight, modern drag wheels.

delivered without many of the usual conveniences, such as heaters and radios. The base price was $5,979, a staggering amount for a Nash.

For 1970 the SC/Rambler gave way to the Rebel Machine, an intermediate supercar that had its own version of AMC's wild red, white, and blue colors (although you could order one in the color of your choice). With a wheelbase of 114 inches, the Rebel Machine made 340 horsepower, the highest horsepower rating ever for an AMC street car. Of course, only American Motors would brag in its advertising about how slow this car was:

Incidentally, if you have delusions of entering the Daytona 500 with the Machine, or challenging people at random, the Machine is not that fast. You should know that.

For instance, it is not as fast on the getaway as a 427 Corvette or a Hemi, but it is faster on the getaway than a Volkswagen, a slow freight train, or your old man's Cadillac.

Odd stuff, but if you liked AMCs, you needed a good sense of humor. The reality was that the Machine was quite capable of keeping up with some pretty impressive pieces. With the 4-speed transmission and 3.54 gears (3.91s were an option), it was capable of mid 14-second ETs.

Production seems to have been 2,326 units, with the first thousand getting the shocking patriotic paint. As mentioned earlier, the body of the car could be any color you liked, but you had to take a flat-black hood and silver stripes.

American Motors wasn't the only company to call on Hurst back then. Grand Spaulding Dodge had it build just under fifty 440-powered Darts in 1968, a full year before Chrysler did it at the factory. (After the muscle car era ended, Grand Spaulding offered its customers the GSS, which was a supercharged 340 Demon.) But it was Oldsmobile that really hit pay dirt with the aftermarket supplier. In Hurst, it found the perfect solution to General Motors' displacement limit—Oldsmobile could not build a 455-powered intermediate, but that didn't mean that someone else couldn't do it for them.

The plan was to build an executive hot rod; to clear up any misconceptions from the start, the Hurst/Olds (H/O) was built from the Cutlass, not the 4-4-2. It was the brainchild of four individuals:

AMERICAN MOTORS

1969 Hurst SC/Rambler

Cu. In.	390
Bore (in.)	4.17
Stroke (in.)	3.57
Compression	10.20:1
Induction	1x4 bbl.
Horsepower/RPM	315/4600
Torque (lbs.-ft.)/RPM	425/3200

1969 Hurst AMX/SS

Cu. In.	390
Bore (in.)	4.17
Stroke (in.)	3.57
Compression	12.30:1
Induction	1x4 bbl.
Horsepower/RPM	340/NA
Torque (lbs.-ft.)/RPM	NA

1970 Rebel Machine

Cu. In.	390
Bore (in.)	4.17
Stroke (in.)	3.57
Compression	12.30:1
Induction	1x4 bbl.
Horsepower/RPM	340/5100
Torque (lbs.-ft.)/RPM	430/3600

The AMC Hurst Rebel machine featured a 340-horsepower 390 engine, the highest-rated engine to ever appear in an AMC street car. This model has the red, white, and blue paint scheme, but you could order the Rebel in several different colors, all with flat-black hoods and silver stripes.

George Hurst and Jack "Doc" Watson from the aftermarket side, and Olds engineers John Beltz and Ted Louckes.

Power came from a modified Toronado 455 that was rated at 390 horses at 5000 rpm and 500 lbs.-ft. of torque at 3600, thanks to a high-lift, long-duration camshaft, free-flowing cylinder heads, a recurved distributor, and a rejetted carb. Naturally, each car was fitted with the under-the-bumper Force-Air Induction system.

Being Oldsmobile hot rods, they were built with automatic transmissions and filled with Hurst Dual Gate shifters. Rounding out the mechanical package were a heavy-duty suspension, rear end assembly with standard 3.91 gears and brakes, a higher-capacity cooling system, and G70x14-inch Goodyear Polyglas tires.

To separate the H/Os from the more plebeian Cutlasses, the new cars sported a Peruvian silver-and-black paint scheme, distinctive Hurst/Olds emblems, and a specially trimmed instrument panel.

Toronado.
The all-car car for the all-man man.

The line of demarcation is drawn. Men on one side. Boys on the other. Cars fall into place. No question which side Toronado takes. Not with that brawny, broad-shouldered look. And that responsive performance from a 455-cubic-inch Rocket V-8, biggest ever built. And that masterful ride and handling, thanks to the superior traction of FRONT-WHEEL DRIVE and torsion-bar suspension. Like we say, Toronado is all man—right down to that man-sized trunk.

The front-wheel-drive youngmobile from Oldsmobile.

GM
MARK OF EXCELLENCE

R16

Hurst/Oldsmobile engines were based on the 455 Rocket engines from the upscale Toronado. Here's a politically incorrect ad for the '69 Toro—notice how Olds touts its front-wheel-drive engineering in bold letters. While FWD is commonplace today, back in the sixties it was high-tech.

Only 515 were ever built, although close to 2,000 were ordered. While a paper shuffle helped fool the brass, the 455s were actually installed on a factory assembly line. This fact flies in the face of legend, which has it that they were assembled at John Demmer's converted foundry on the corner of Ballard and Oakland in Lansing, Michigan. The work done at Demmer Special Machinery included paint and installation of trim, such as the wooden dash.

(According to Doc Watson, in addition to the 515 H/Os made available to the general public, there were also four built with manual transmissions—one for him, another for John Demmer's son, and two others.)

Snarls Softly

Because of its success with consumers, the Hurst/Olds was brought back in 1969. The paint scheme was changed to white with gold stripes, and in a real departure the under-the-bumper Force-Air setup was removed in favor of a more traditional dual-scooped "mailbox" hood. Tire size was increased to F60x15 and horsepower was decreased by 10.

Still, the folks at *Super Stock & Drag Illustrated* raved. Testing an air-conditioned model with 3.23 gears in their July 1969 issue, they went a somewhat disappointing 14.87 at 97 mph. They were much happier with a non-air-conditioned car that had 3.42 gears and went a much quicker 14.20 at 98.50 mph. As its ads said, it "snarls softly and carries a big stick."

Drag racing results, however, were just a small part of the story. *SS&DI* waxed poetic about the Hurst/Olds' ride, handling, and comfort. And of the vehicle's new looks, they wrote, "At rest, the H/O is a beautiful piece of automotive sculpture." Production increased to 906, plus six prototypes and two convertibles.

As it turned out, the two companies hooked up once more during the muscle car era—in 1972 when the Hurst/Olds was picked to pace the Indianapolis 500. Again painted Cameo White and Firefrost Gold, it was propelled by a 300-net-horse 455 with ram induction. Only an automatic transmission was offered.

Snakes Alive

What Carroll Shelby and his crew did with the Mustang GT350 was nothing short of miraculous. Here was a car based on the lowly Ford Falcon that, by the time Shelby American was done with it, was spanking the Corvette Sting Ray in SCCA B-Production road racing.

While the addition of horsepower was integral to this transformation, horsepower alone did not do the trick. Fully adjustable Koni shocks were used at all four corners and the front suspension geometry was slightly revised: the stock front sway bar was replaced with a beefy, 1-inch-diameter unit. To limit axle hop in the rear, the kind of traction bars usually found on a drag car were utilized. A Galaxie 9-inch rear with a Detroit Locker limited slip differential was standard, but this noisy differential was the source of so much controversy it was dropped for 1966. Much larger than stock 11-inch Kelsey-Hayes vented disc brakes were used up front and

Because the '68 Hurst/Olds proved so popular, the '69 model (top) was produced. Instead of the traditional below-the-bumper Olds Force-Air induction system, the '69 H/O used a twin-scooped hood to feed air to the carb. The last in the line of "real" Hurst/Olds performance machines was the 1972 model (above). (That year also happened to be the last for an intermediate GM convertible.)

Opposite: When the big-block Shelby Mustangs became available in 1967 (above), most of them came standard with 428s, although some came with 427s. The popularity of the big block shifted attention away from the smaller-engined GT350 (below). Top: The 1969 Shelbys barely resembled their Mustang counterparts. Because they offered little or no performance advantage over their Mach 1, Boss, and GT brethren, Ford had to take advantage of the Shelby name and image to boost sales. Above: The Shelby insignia from the '69 Cobra GT500 fastback.

10-inch rear drums were fitted with 2½-inch-wide sintered metallic linings.

To take full advantage of the chassis's capabilities, a Monte Carlo bar and export brace were installed under the hood—effectively keeping the front end from flexing. The slow steering was speeded up by lengthening the Pitman arm 1 inch.

It held the road tenaciously and its side-exiting exhausts with glasspack mufflers were pure rock 'n' roll. Buoyed by the GT350's stripes and Shelby emblems, this new 'Stang was an instant sensation.

Which, of course, ultimately led to its being watered down. Purists cringed when in 1966 things like the backseat reappeared and the battery found its way back under the hood, but Shelby and Ford were both in business to make money. First-year production was only 562 units, which included thirty-five competition "R" models and nine drag cars.

For 1966 the GT350 was slightly more civilized (an automatic transmission was optional), but it was still a warrior. A Paxton supercharger became an option at $670. But the ultimate coup for Shelby was Hertz Rent A Car's order for one thou-sand Shelby Mustangs, which were dubbed GT350H. Almost all of these cars were equipped with automatic transmissions and, there were rules governing who could rent them, yet many came back stinking of burnt rubber and bearing the scars of organized competition.

As the Mustang got larger in 1967 and the trend toward big-block power grew, it came as little surprise when the 428 Shelby appeared in 1967. What was surprising was how quickly the car was moving away from its roots as a thinly disguised racer. For 1967 Shelby had Chuck McHose and Pete Stacey substantially alter the Mustang's appearance.

A fiberglass nose extension gave the car a substantially meaner look. Mounted in the center of the grille were two 7-inch driving lights, which became a source of controversy. Most '67s had them mounted together in the center of the grille. Not only was this deemed illegal in some states, but it also caused overheating in some cars. The solution was to separate them, moving them to the outer extremities of the grille. A functional fiberglass hood was standard.

FORD/SHELBY MUSTANGS

1965

Cu. In.	289
Bore (in.)	4.00
Stroke (in.)	2.87
Compression	10.50:1
Induction	1x4 bbl.
Horsepower/RPM	306/6000
Torque (lbs.-ft.)/RPM	329/4200

1966

Cu. In.	289
Bore (in.)	4.00
Stroke (in.)	2.87
Compression	10.50:1
Induction	1x4 bbl.
Horsepower/RPM	306/6000
Torque (lbs.-ft.)/RPM	329/4200

1967

Cu. In.	289
Bore (in.)	4.00
Stroke (in.)	2.87
Compression	10.50:1
Induction	1x4 bbl.
Horsepower/RPM	306/6000
Torque (lbs.-ft.)/RPM	329/4200

1967 (cont.)

Cu. In.	427	428
Bore (in.)	4.23	4.13
Stroke (in.)	3.78	3.98
Compression	11.00:1	10.50:1
Induction	2x4 bbl.	2x4 bbl.
Horsepower/RPM	425/6000	355/5400
Torque (lbs.-ft.)/RPM	476/3400	420/3700

1968

Cu. In.	302	
Bore (in.)	4.00	
Stroke (in.)	3.00	
Compression	10.00:1	
Induction	1x4 bbl.	
Horsepower/RPM	250/4800	335/5200*
Torque (lbs.-ft.)/RPM	318/3200	325/3200

*With optional Paxton supercharger

1968 (cont.)

Cu. In.	427	428	
Bore (in.)	4.23	4.13	
Stroke (in.)	3.78	3.98	
Compression	11.60:1	10.50:1	10.70:1
Induction	1x4 bbl.	1x4 bbl.	1x4 bbl.
Horsepower/RPM	400/5600	360/5400	335/5400
Torque (lbs.-ft.)/RPM	460/3200	420/3200	445/3400

1969/1970

Cu. In.	351	428
Bore (in.)	4.00	4.13
Stroke (in.)	3.50	3.98
Compression	10.70:1	10.70:1
Induction	1x4 bbl.	1x4 bbl.
Horsepower/RPM	290/4800	335/5400
Torque (lbs.-ft.)/RPM	385/3200	445/3400

Side scoops for the brakes (these scoops had first appeared in 1966) and passenger compartment were mounted behind the doors and on the sides of the roof, respectively, and a fiberglass decklid with integral spoiler was used. But the sharpest trick was the use of dechromed Cougar taillights, which ran practically the width of the car.

The power plant for the Mustang GT350 remained the modified high-performance 289, but a special 428 was used in the big-block model, which was crowned the GT500. Most of these came with a Shelbyized version of the Police Interceptor engine, with dual 600 cfm Holleys on an aluminum medium-riser intake, a heavy-duty cam, and 10.5:1 compression—good for 355 hp and 420 lbs. ft. of torque.

A handful of other GT500s came with the 425-horse 427, but the exact number is not known. Even with the "lesser" 428, these snakes flew. I had the opportunity to test one a few years back and it posted a 0–60 time of 5.4 seconds and a quarter-mile ET of 13.76 at 102.82.

Unlike the '65 Shelby Mustang, which had side-exiting exhausts, the '69 had twin pipes that ran out through the center of the rear valance.

In drag-race tune (race tires, open exhaust), 427/425-horse Camaros like this '69 Yenko were capable of 11-second ETs at the track. Combined with their limited production, this makes them extraordinarily valuable today.

For 1968 Ford took over Shelby Mustang production and things pretty much went south from there. Production moved to Livonia, Michigan, where the cars were built by the A.O. Smith Company. The emphasis was now placed on luxury rather than performance. The high-winding 289 was replaced by an anemic 302 4-barrel (it really needed the optional supercharger). The 428, though rated at 5 more horsepower, came with one less carburetor. When the 428 Cobra Jet was released in mid-1968, this engine became the only big block in the Shelby, and the Shelby, previously designated GT500, came to be called GT500KR, for "King of the Road." For the first time, you could get air-conditioning. The interior was awash in woodgrain trim, and a convertible model was an option. Still desirable and still very fast, it was, however, a Shelby in name only.

By 1969 the GT350 and GT500 were totally restyled and barely recognizable as Mustangs. The fiberglass front end hinted at what the Mustang would look like in 1971, while '65 Thunderbird taillights were used out back. It was the least "Shelby" of all the cars that bore his name. The 351 4-barrel with 290 horsepower was standard in the GT350. It differed from the production Mustang engine only in that it had an aluminum intake and Cobra valve covers.

Big-block lovers got the same 428 Cobra Jet found in regular Mach 1 Mustangs—in fact, the Competition suspension and rear axle were the same, too. It's sad to think that a Shelby Mustang would have a heavy-duty suspension as an option, but such was the state of the nation.

Approximately 789 Shelbys were left over after the '69 model year. These were rebadged, altered

slightly, and sold as 1970 models. Not surprisingly, this spelled the end of Shelby production.

Bigger Is Better

No one was hurt more than Chevrolet by the General Motors edict limiting cubic inches in midsize cars to 400. Chevy was supposed to be the performance division and it was hamstrung by a harebrained corporate decision. Ford was pumping out 427 and 428 Fairlanes and Mustangs, and you could get up to 440 cubic inches in a compact-size Dodge Dart, but a 427 Chevelle? Heavens, no!

But as in any good capitalistic society, GM's myopia led to great fortune for those with the presence of mind to build what it would not. One per-

Barely known then or now, the Fred Gibb Chevrolet/Dick Harrell 427 Novas of 1968 were fearsome performers—every bit the screamers that the more well-known cars from Motion Performance and Yenko Chevrolet were.

son who saw the possible gold at the end of the rainbow was Joel Rosen of Motion Performance in Baldwin, New York.

"As soon as the Camaro came out in 1967, it was obvious there was a market for a 427 version—at least to me it was obvious," Rosen said. He teamed up with Baldwin Chevrolet and began ordering 396/375-horse cars (because the solid-lifter engines were so easy to sell after the swap) and installing 425-horse L72 427 engines in them.

"The basic package went for about $4,000. It was cheap; that's why it went over so well," he recalled. "The original concept was to build a plain Jane sleeper. Then it was up to the customer if he wanted to order a different carburetor, hood, traction bars, etc."

So popular were the Camaros that by 1968 Rosen and Baldwin Chevrolet began to do heavily

modified Corvettes; the following year they were followed by 427 Novas, Chevelles, and special Biscaynes. Rosen, however, wasn't the only person profiting from these kinds of swaps. Don Yenko, through his Chevy dealership in Canonsburg, Pennsylvania, was doing similar things in 1967, as were Fred Gibb Chevrolet, Berger Chevrolet, Nickey Chevrolet, Dana Chevrolet, and others.

The demand was so great that by the '69 model year (and possibly earlier), Yenko had worked out a clever deal to have one hundred cars built on a factory assembly line through use of a Central Office Production Order (COPO). Eventually, another 101 cars were ordered by Yenko, and other astute dealerships got in on the action as well. Though no one knows for sure how many, it is believed that approximately three hundred more went to these other dealers.

Don't get the idea that the stock 375-horse Camaros were slugs. They were extremely potent. As the decade wore on, though, 396 cubes weren't always enough to compete with some of the modified street pounders. That's when you needed the heavy artillery. *Super Stock & Drag Illustrated* tested a '69 Yenko Sports Cars 427 Camaro in its July 1969 issue and the results were mind-boggling. The only deviation from a production 427/425 engine was a set of open Doug Thorley headers. With 8-inch-wide M&H slicks and 4.10 gears, the Camaro rolled to an 11.94 at 114.50 mph.

Research has shown that COPO Chevelles were also available in 1969. But that is only part of the story; recently discovered documentation has shown that Yenko may have ordered and sold 1968 COPO Camaros. Perhaps the only person

who knew for sure was Don Yenko, and he died in a plane crash years ago. Rosen does not remember any '68 COPO cars, but he doesn't rule out the possibility of their existence: "They might have let one or two slip out; that's always a possibility. But I never saw one."

As for the 427 Novas, Rosen wasn't the only person to build or sell them either. Yenko and Gibb did, too. Blindingly fast, they were not easy cars to drive, and some insurance companies flatly refused to handle them. For this, Yenko had a solution. In 1970 he produced a number of Chevy IIs with the potent but lightweight LT-1 Corvette motor. Known as the Yenko Deuce, this car came straight from the factory (via a Fleet Order, not a COPO) with the LT-1 and a 12-bolt rear with 4.10 gears. It should come as little surprise that with 370 horsepower, it gave you mind-altering acceleration. These cars were produced only in 1970, and a total of 176 were built.

Royal Flush

If you were a fan of Pontiac performance in the 1960s, then Ace Wilson's Royal Pontiac dealership needs no introduction. If you weren't, let's just say it was as close to heaven as a Tin Indian lover could get. Royal successfully raced Pontiacs, tuned them to a razor's edge, and sold engine parts and kits for them. Mention that your GTO had Royal's "Bobcat treatment" and others knew yours was not a car to be taken lightly.

For the most part Royal's Bobcat workover meant that your cylinder heads were completely worked, Polylocks were used to allow you to adjust

When Don Yenko produced 427 Novas (top) in 1969, the insurance companies balked. Because they were so powerful and so light, many owners were denied insurance. This led Yenko to build the more civilized Yenko Deuce in 1970, which packed the Z/28's new 360-horsepower 350 engine. Because of its drag racing exploits, Royal Pontiac of Royal Oak, Michigan, was recognized in the sixties as one of the premier Poncho tuners. When Ace Wilson's boys worked their magic on a car like this '65 GTO convertible (above), that car would be pretty tough to beat in the stoplight Grand Prix.

CHRYSLER/HURST HEMI DARTS & BARRACUDAS	
1968	
Cu. In.	426
Bore (in.)	4.25
Stroke (in.)	3.75
Compression	12.50:1
Induction	2x4 bbl.
Horsepower/RPM	not rated
Torque (lbs.-ft.)/RPM	not rated

your rocker arms, ignitions received a heavy-duty condenser and points, and your carb (or carbs) was tweaked so it worked like it should. Thinner head gaskets were used to bring up compression and headers were more than likely added as well. A Bobcatted GTO Judge tested in the April '69 *SS&DI* was able to cover the quarter-mile in 12.77 seconds at 109.95 mph with open headers and racing slicks.

Jim Wangers, Pontiac's public relations guru, was a Royal drag racer in the early sixties and set numerous national records in Royal's cars. Naturally, that meant the dealership was often called upon when magazine test cars needed a little help. It was a wonderful arrangement that helped sell thousands of supercars.

Like Yenko, Baldwin-Motion, and the other muscle car customizers, Royal saw fit to transplant breathed-upon 428 Pontiac engines in Firebirds and Goats. These were serious automobiles, capable of blowing off most anything you were likely to encounter on the highway.

One can only imagine how much money General Motors threw away because of its refusal to ditch the 400-cubic-inch limit before 1970.

A-Bombs

Earlier, we mentioned that outside influences were responsible for the creation of some of the best high-speed muscle car hybrids. In the case of the '68 Hemi Darts and Barracudas, this influence was Super Stock drag racing. Chrysler wanted to rule this particular world and decided that a no-holds-barred, race-only brawler was the only answer. This being the case, it turned to Hurst Performance, which converted eighty-three Dodge and seventy-two Plymouth A-bodies into race-Hemi bombs.

What made up these strip-only terrors, which still rule Super Stock more than a quarter century after they were built? They were lightened with fiberglass front fenders, hoods, and scoops. The doors were acid-dipped. Front bumpers were made out of thinner-gauge steel than production models. Chemcor .080-inch-thick side glass was used—thinner and lighter than stock.

The engines were similar to the production Street Hemi, with that engine's cam and cylinder heads. The major differences were 12.5:1 compression pistons and a cross-ram, dual-quad intake.

Befitting a race car, rear seats, rearview mirrors, radios, and heaters were deleted, thus subtracting more weight. For better weight distribution, the battery, which was larger than stock, was moved to the trunk. Instead of regular Dart or Barracuda buckets, a pair of A-100 van seats on aluminum tracks was used.

The second step was to ship the A-bodies and their assorted pieces to Hurst for assembly. Hurst installed the massive Hemi and the rest of the drivetrain, and bolted on the lightweight body parts and interior. The rear wheelwells were slightly enlarged on the Darts.

Once assembled, these cars were either picked up at Hurst by customers or shipped to dealers. Since they were destined to be race cars, they were shipped in primer. In the good old days, they ran 10.30s on contemporary rubber. Today, they are close to breaking into the 8-second zone.

Automobiles don't come any quicker than the '68 Hurst Hemi Darts (right) and their Plymouth Barracuda cousins. They have been the top performers in the Super Stock A class for over twenty-five years. This is how they looked when delivered from the Hurst foundry; note the enlarged rear wheelwells and fiberglass front clips.

Chapter 6

Racing Improves the Breed

I was cruising in my Sting Ray late one night When an XKE pulled up on the right He rolled down the window of his shiny new Jag And challenged me then and there to a drag...

—"Dead Man's Curve," by Jan and Dean

Above right: Henry Ford (standing) with racing pioneer Barney Oldfield and the land speed record–setting "999." A legitimate case could be made that Ford was the original hot rodder. He used racing to garner publicity for his fledgling car company (this trick is still used today). Opposite: One result of the Ford Motor Company's involvement in racing over the years was the '70 Boss 302 Mustang, which was built for SCCA Trans-Am racing.

It was a lesson learned by auto moguls long before the muscle car era: speed sells. Racing had been instrumental in the success of many of the earliest car companies, and it has been a part of the Ford Motor Company's development and marketing strategies for as long as that organization has been in business. Henry Ford, who was himself a dyed-in-the-wool speed freak, built numerous racing contraptions, and on January 12, 1904, he and codriver Spider Huff set the land speed record at 91.37 mph.

This was truly flying without leaving the ground—not to mention more than 14 mph faster than the previous record, which had been set by the French. Power for the car, known as "999," came from a 1,156-cubic-inch 4-banger (talk about your big blocks!). This kind of derring-do garnered huge newspaper headlines all over the world—terrific publicity.

This lesson was not lost on Henry's competition—not then and not now. The old saying "Racing improves the breed" was gospel, whether it was Barney Oldfield or Rusty Wallace doing the driving. Back around the turn of the century, cars were oddities—an unknown, often unreliable quantity. Race-proven performance and durability were big selling points.

Altered States

How far would car manufacturers go to win races in the sixties? As far as necessary. Ford built its A/FX Cyclones and Fairlanes, lightweight Galaxies, and Single Overhead Cam engines; Chevrolet had its Mk. II Mystery Engines and ZL-1 Corvettes and Camaros. Pontiac drilled holes in its frames to lighten the Catalina (hence the name Swiss Cheese car). And Chrysler had its two-percenters and altered-wheelbase (AWB) cars. Long forgotten by many enthusiasts, the two-percent cars predated the more radical AWB machines that would lead to the coining of the term "Funny Car." These cars first appeared (in the very limited number of four) in late 1964. The two-percenters had their wheelbases altered, by—you guessed it—two percent because NHRA rules allowed you to change the wheelbase by this much in Factory Experimental.

Why go to all this trouble? Traction. The tire technology of the day was not nearly as advanced as the horsepower technology. By moving the front wheels forward, engineers were able to get better weight transfer and increased traction.

For the 1965 NHRA Winternationals in Pomona, California, Chrysler built four '65 two percent cars. The well-known drivers given the first factory rides were Jim Thornton (Ramchargers) and Roger "Color Me Gone" Lindamood in Dodge Coronets, and Tommy Grove (the Melrose Missile) and Al Eckstrand (Hamilton Motors–sponsored Golden Commandos) in Plymouths. The cars had lightweight body panels and structures, but retained the standard wheelbase.

These first AWB machines were not much more than transition vehicles. After the Winternats, Chrysler, operating under the erroneous assumption that the NHRA would abandon its two-percent rule in Factory Experimental, built six Dodges and six Plymouths—three of which were converted two-percenters—with radically altered wheelbases. A 15-inch section of the unitbody was cut out behind the front seats and the rear subframe sections and the back axle were moved forward a like distance. Finally, through the use of a special crossmember and underpinnings, the front wheels were moved forward 10 inches.

When these cars were brought to the strip, NHRA representatives would not budge, and the vehicles were factored into one of the altered classes. They were also legal for exhibition runs and match races, which were very profitable and offered great visibility. And they also found a legal home in the AHRA, where they did quite well.

Either way, the AWB machines' place in history is secure. They not only gave rise to a new piece of vocabulary, but also made a unique statement about the lengths to which the factories would go to be competitive.

Cigar-chomping Dick Landy drove this altered-wheelbase Dodge Coronet (left) in 1965. In their quest for better traction, Chrysler engineers moved the rear wheels forward 15 inches and the front wheels 10. Classified by the NHRA as Altereds instead of Factory Experimentals, these vehicles enjoyed more success in the AHRA (American Hot Rod Association) and on the match-racing circuit than in NHRA and NASCAR competition. The injected Hemi engines (above) were a radical departure from even the usual Super Stock race motors.

During the muscle car era, Ford said to hell with the 1957 AMA racing ban, and immersed itself completely in every form of motorsport. It also adopted a new slogan—"Total Performance"—and began attacking every type of competition under the sun.

Meanwhile, other carmakers became similarly engaged. Both the NHRA and NASCAR had rules that required race car engines and body styles to be at least based on production models. This gave rise to the Hemi Dodges and Plymouths, Boss 429 Mustangs, ZL-1 Camaros, and a plethora of other unbelievable machinery.

Among the best of the early 1960s race cars were the Super Duty Pontiacs, Z-11 Chevrolets, and Thunderbolt Fords. While they were responsible for escalating cubic inches in street cars, it wasn't until Big Bill France forced Chrysler to build a number of production Hemis in 1966 that the whole scene got a whole lot hairier. Who could have realized that in less than five years the automotive world would be as hairy as any Haight Ashbury hippie?

It wouldn't just be Hemi Mopars that arrived that year; the W-30 Oldsmobile and 427 Fairlane were also born of this marriage of street and track. Neither of these, however, would make the kind of impact that the Chrysler machines did.

Flying Elephants

Street Hemi. A car name that means power and intimidation. Much has been written over the years about these incredible beasts, some of it true, some incorrect, some hyperbolic, but all contributing to their myth and legend.

Part of the lore surrounding the Hemi, which was known as the Elephant, is based on the results of early road tests. It didn't matter much which magazine you picked up—*Car and Driver, Car Life, Super Stock & Drag Illustrated,* or *Car Craft*—the Hemi would usually hold the crown for quickest quarter-miler (Cobras and Corvettes excluded).

While Dodge expected the '68 Charger to be a world-beater in NASCAR, just the opposite turned out to be true. It wasn't nearly as aerodynamic as the engineers had hoped, and it won only five races that year.

To improve aerodynamics, a number of changes were made and a special 1969 model known as the Charger 500 was introduced. Aerodynamic aids included a flush grille with exposed headlights, and a flush, sloping rear window replaced the standard unit. Further differentiation came from a bumblebee stripe wrapped around the trunk and rear fenders with the 500 designation and more aerodynamic windshield moldings.

A headline in the April 1969 issue of *SS&DI* read "Caution: This Car Could Be Hazardous to Your Mind." The magazine's reviewers were impressed by the Hemi Charger's performance (13.79 at 104.51), but lamented that the 4-speed car was virtually impossible to launch on standard street rubber. While between thirty-two and thirty-five Charger 500s were built with the Hemi, about 392 (U.S. sales) were built with the 375 horse 440 Magnum. They are seldom seen today.

The Charger 500, however, was just a stop-gap measure. Ford was involved in the development of its own aerodynamic warriors. It developed the droop-nose Torino Talladega and the Mercury Cyclone Spoiler II for use on the highbanks, where these cars were generally 5 mph faster than the Mopar. Like the Charger 500, both of the Ford Motor Company vehicles had flush grilles with exposed headlights. Unlike the nose on the Dodge, however, the noses on the Ford and Mercury cars were extended some 5 inches and dropped down. With the better aerodynamics inherent in Ford's fastback design, it was back to the drawing board for the Chrysler engineers.

What they came back with was perhaps the most unusual-looking street car since the Tucker. The Dodge Charger Daytona had a wing that measured close to 24 inches in height (it worked lower, but this was how high it had to be in order for you to be able to open the trunk), a pointy steel nose cone with hideaway headlights that extended the body nearly 18 inches, and the same flush rear window used on the Charger 500. The front fenders had scoops on them that were functional on the race cars, allowing the teams to lower the bodies without having the front tires rub.

While the Ford teams had been pitching a shutout on the long tracks (one mile or more in

The droop-nose styling of the '69 Torino Talladega (shown in street trim) and its Cyclone Spoiler II cousins gave Ford an aerodynamic advantage over the Dodge Charger 500 in NASCAR super-speedway competition.

Top: The K&K Insurance Charger Daytona (#71) driven by Bobby Isaac was the first NASCAR stocker to qualify at over 200 mph. Above: When the Charger 500 didn't meet its maker's expectations, Dodge pulled out all the stops and built the Charger Daytona (shown). This car's long, sloping nose and tall rear wing helped give it great stability at high speeds, plus the aerodynamic capabilities to run over 200 mph for the first time.

length) against the 500, things changed once the Daytona debuted. In qualifying at the new Talladega super speedway, "Chargin'" Charlie Glotzbach pushed his Daytona to a 199.466 mph lap—the fastest ever to that point by a full 9 mph. When a strike before the race (over tire-safety concerns) kept most of the big-name pilots on the sidelines, Richard Brickhouse found himself behind the wheel of Glotzbach's ride. He also found himself in the winner's circle that day, ahead of Jim Vandiver in a Charger 500 and Bobby Isaac in another Daytona.

(Isaac scored the first "nonstrike" super-speedway win in a Daytona at the 1969 season finale.)

Production for the Daytona was either 501 or 503 (U.S. sales), and approximately fifty more were sold north of the border. Most were standard 440 4-barrel cars and the remainder were Hemi-powered.

As noted earlier, Ford's answer to the need for increased aerodynamics on NASCAR's super speedways was answered by the Torino Talladega and the Mercury Cyclone Spoiler II. Since Ford

had to play by the same rules as Chrysler, it too was required to build five hundred each of the Talladega and Spoiler II for the street. (In the case of the Mercury, Ford Motor Company did not live up to this requirement.)

Unlike the Daytona, the Ford and Mercury aerodynamic cars were not that dramatically different from their standard fastback siblings. While the Talladegas had rerolled rocker panels to let the cars be lowered on the track, they were bone stock from the A-pillars back.

The only interchangeable parts on the Talladegas and Spoiler IIs were the grille and bumper. The nose extensions were made of two stampings welded together, some of which were done at Holman & Moody. These were grafted onto shortened standard fenders. All the Talladegas were done at the Torino's Atlanta assembly plant and the Mercurys were built in their usual Lorain, Ohio, plant.

You could only get 428 Cobra Jet (not Super Cobra Jet) power in the Talladegas; some—and they were the only non-drag pack Fords built that got them—had oil coolers. They also came standard with staggered rear shocks. All were equipped with C-6 automatics with column shifters and 3.25 gears in a 31-spline axle.

The street Spoiler IIs were outfitted for less performance. The sole power plant was the 290-horse 351 4-barrel. All had the FMX automatic transmission and 3.25 gears, but not the heavy-duty axle.

The most labor-intensive piece on the car was the front bumper. It was made from a heavily re-worked Torino rear bumper that was cut three times, rewelded, narrowed, filled in, and rechromed.

Every Talladega had a cloth-insert bench seat and the only available option was an AM radio. Color choices were Presidential Blue, Royal Maroon, and Wimbledon White.

Spoiler IIs came through either as white-and-blue Dan Gurney models or white-and-red Cale Yarborough models. Befitting their more luxurious Mercury image, they came standard with all-vinyl bench interiors (Gurney's were blue and Yarborough's were red). The decals that came with the package were in the trunk awaiting dealer installation. Finally, the Spoiler II's rear wing was unique to that car.

According to its records, Ford produced a total of 745 Talladegas, including prototypes, but it is believed that many more were actually produced. To homologate them for NASCAR, Ford claimed it built 513 Spoiler II Cyclones, but no less an authority than Ralph Moody himself said that Mercury did not make nearly that many. The actual number is believed to be 352 or so, and only half of that number are known to exist.

The rear wing on the '70 Plymouth Superbird (top and above) and '69 Dodge Daytona worked just a well in a shorter version. It had to be as tall as it was on production cars to allow the trunks to open.

Bird Is the Word

To lure Richard Petty back and try again to be competitive, Plymouth launched a wing car of its own in 1970. The Road Runner Superbird, while similar in appearance to the Daytona, was actually quite different. It had a unique nose cone that was fitted to '70 Dodge Coronet front fenders (it also used a Coronet hood). The rear wing was more upright than that of the Daytona and the rear window was different. To cover the battle scars from where the roof was reworked to fit this window, all street cars came with vinyl roofs.

For power, you had a choice of the 375-horse 440 4-barrel, 390-horse 440 6-barrel, or 425-horse Street Hemi. Bench seats were standard, but buckets were available. Production figures are also cloudy. Some historians say 1,920 Superbirds were built; Chrysler Historical claims 1,935; others say 1,971.

Because of their oddball styling, many 'Birds languished on dealer lots for up to two years. They sure did work on the race track, though. Richard Petty entered forty races in 1970 and won eighteen of them, finishing in the Top Five twenty-seven times and in the Top Ten in thirty-one events.

So whose aerodynamic cars were the best? Well, contrary to what some people remember, it was the Fords and Mercurys that did best. Over the two-year period in which they were allowed to race, Talladegas won 49 out of 102 races. On tracks of one mile or more (excluding road courses), the Talladega registered fourteen wins in 1969 and 1970, the Spoiler II eight, the Superbird seven, the Daytona six, and the Charger 500 one.

Playing with Blocks

Of course, everyone knows Chevrolet was not racing in the sixties. That's why it went to all the trouble of building sixty-nine Camaros in 1969 with the all-aluminum (and frightfully expensive) ZL-1 427 engine. According to Edward J. Cunneen's book *COPO Camaros and Chevelles: Facts, Figures, Documentation*, fifty of these machines were ordered by Fred Gibb for his dealership (remember, this was the number necessary to qualify the cars for NHRA competition).

Using the 9560 COPO order, other dealerships combined to order another nineteen for the final production number.

While aluminum heads were available as an option on the 396 and were helpful for paring unnecessary weight, the ZL-1 with its aluminum block brought the weight down to about that of a small-block Camaro.

The first two cars left the Norwood, Ohio, plant on January 1, 1969, and the following forty-eight were delivered in March. Gibb was stunned when he found out that the optional engine cost $4,160. This put the list price of the cars over $7,200. He convinced Chevrolet to take back twenty of them, and as Cunneen mentions in his book, they were redistributed to other dealers.

Gibb probably never realized playing with blocks could be so expensive.

The End Is Near

While 1970 is regarded as the peak of the muscle car era, so too was it the last year in which the factories built cars specifically for homologation purposes. The '69 and '70 Boss Mustangs housed the Boss 302 and Boss 429 engines for use in Trans-Am and NASCAR, respectively. The '71 Boss 351 Mustang, which used one of the greatest Ford engines of all time, was a simply outstanding street machine. Everyone except AMC was pulling out of racing. It was too costly and the advent of stricter and stricter pollution laws meant the manufacturers needed all their resources and engineering talent to continue development.

Besides, the day of the true factory supercar was ending and carmakers knew it. Sales had fallen off as insurance premiums had risen. The 1973 Arab oil embargo was the final nail in the coffin. When the price of petroleum doubled, there were few consumers who remained willing to put up with 6 mpg fuel economy. On came the imports, while Chevy developed the Vega and Ford created the Pinto.

Is it any wonder that muscle cars are so sought after today?

The ultimate ponycars from perennial rivals Chevrolet and Ford were the 1969 ZL-1 Camaro (above), which had an all-aluminum 427 engine, and the 1969 and 1970 (right) Boss 429 Mustangs, with their Hemi-headed Shotgun engines. These Mustangs were built to homologate the engine for NASCAR competition, where it was installed in Torinos and Cyclones.

Chapter 7

Dream On

*Well, she got her
daddy's car and she
cruised through the
hamburger stand now
Seems she forgot all
about the library like
she told her old man
now
And with her radio
blasting she goes
cruisin' just as fast as
she can now
And she'll have fun, fun,
fun till her daddy takes
the T-bird away...*

—"Fun, Fun, Fun,"
by the Beach Boys

AMC styling boss Richard Teague tried to catch the same lightning in a bottle with the AMX/3 (above right) that Chevrolet did with the '53 Corvette (opposite) twenty years earlier. It wasn't to be. Here's Teague (left) with Giotti Bizzarini, the Italian engineer hired by AMC to build its dream car, and the magnificent AMX/3 in Rome in 1973.

Fantasies play an important role in the life of every human being. Whether they involve winning the lottery, running off to a tropical island with the man or woman of one's dreams, or designing your own muscle car, everybody has them. Unfortunately, however, few of us get to realize our fantasies.

If you are an automobile designer or engineer, though, you don't have to be satisfied with keeping your dreams in your head. You get paid for letting your wildest automotive fantasies come to life, either on paper or, if you get really lucky, as a show car/experimental. The biggest thrill is to see one of your concepts become a production reality.

While fantasy cars have been around since General Motors introduced the Buick Y-Job in 1938, it was during the muscle car era that some of the finest and most influential dream cars came to be. Whether you want to call them "dream cars," "concept cars," or "experimentals," their basic raison d'être is the same: tantalize the buying public with futuristic designs, showcase cutting-edge technology, and test the public's acceptance of new ideas. At the same time, these automobiles can turn those who see them into potential customers for current models.

The first concept car to make it almost intact as a production model was the Chevrolet Corvette, which first appeared in January 1953 at the GM Motorama at the Waldorf-Astoria in New York City. Public reaction was so favorable that it was rushed into production by June of that year. The introduction of the 'Vette marked the beginning of a love affair between the American public and a two-seat sports car that has lasted more than forty years.

The Corvette had a lightweight fiberglass body, which was revolutionary in its day; it was also a two-seat sports car. This was nothing unusual if you lived in England or Italy, but in North America, it was a fairly off-the-wall idea. It is believed that over four million people viewed the Corvette as it made the Motorama rounds in the United States and Canada that year, and that their acceptance of the new car convinced Chevrolet to forge ahead with production.

A similar case developed with the Mustang in 1962. Ford had already given the go-ahead to build the four-place sporty car, but they could not figure out how best to generate excitement for it among the media and the car-buying public. In the end, Ford decided to produce a couple of show cars: the Mustang and the Mustang II.

The Mustang, which debuted at the U.S. Grand Prix in Watkins Glen, New York, in October 1962, was a traditional sports car in almost every sense of the word. It was small, weighing in at a mere 1,148 pounds, had a tiny 1.5-liter V4 power plant that produced a modest 109 hp, and seated two people. And like most futuristic show cars, it incorporated a host of high-tech goodies that would not see production for over a decade, if ever—rack and pinion steering, midship engine configuration, an aluminum body, retractable headlights, and a hideaway front license plate.

The Mustang was received enthusiastically by *Car and Driver* in its September 1962 issue. "The Mustang shows what Ford Engineering and Styling can do when given a chance," it said.

Later in 1962 the Mustang gave way to the less radical Mustang II, which gave away the size and much of the styling of the soon-to-be-released production model. This prototype was a four-seater with bucket seats up front, a bench seat in the rear, and a removable fiberglass hardtop. Among the items that made it into production were the C-shaped side scoops, which lasted from 1965 to 1968 and from 1974 to 1978, and have been brought back on the 1994 Mustang; a deep, oval-shaped grille; and 3-bar vertical tail lamps.

A Pontiac Monte Carlo?

One of the more entertaining aspects of the dream car circuit is studying the names that turn up. Buick hatched the name LeSabre—one it still uses today—in 1951 on a two-place luxury sports car. And Firebird, Dart, Wildcat, and Futura are just a few of the other nameplates that originated in the land of experimentals.

One of the more curious show cars of the early sixties was the '62 Pontiac Tempest Monte Carlo. Sporting a name that would show up on a Chevrolet personal luxury car nine years later, the Tempest Monte Carlo was a slick little two-seater that sported such niceties as a supercharged 4-cylinder engine, bucket seats with pronounced side bolsters, and a cut-down windshield. And Oldsmobile had its own, perhaps nicer, version of the Monte Carlo. Dubbed the X-215, this car was based on a turbocharged Jetfire.

Actually, Pontiac was one of the more active GM divisions in the concept car department. Also debuting in 1962 was the Grand Prix X-400, which not only was supercharged but also sported some of the first rectangular headlights ever seen on an American car. This model, whose roots were in the X-400s of 1959 to 1961, was updated over the next couple of years, as Pontiac engineers played with vertical headlight concepts and more supercharged V8s.

Of greater interest to muscle car enthusiasts, however, was the experimental version of the GTO trotted out by Pontiac in 1964. While similar in appearance to the production car, it sported rectangular headlamps, side-exiting exhaust pipes,

While sharing the look of the Tempest sport coupe (above), the Tempest Monte Carlo (top) was just one of Pontiac's two-seat dream machines that never saw production. Only one—the Fiero, which debuted in the 1984 model year—would ever see production. After a brief success, the Fiero died a shameful death, plagued by poor quality and countless recalls.

chrome reverse rims, and a lowered suspension. Much of the exterior brightwork (for instance, the Goat's grille emblem) was either toned down or removed. The aim of the experimental GTO was to draw attention to the production car.

Dodge gave people a glimpse into its future in 1964 with the Charger show car. This vehicle was a two-seat version of the '64 Dodge Polara and it featured all the usual concept car tricks of the day: cut-down windscreen, roll bar with built-in headrest fairings, "lake" pipes, and mag wheels. It also bore a resemblance to the Dodge Charger Funny Cars, thanks to a very similar twin-scooped hood. Power came from a 426 wedge.

Then came the Charger II. Unlike its forerunner, the Charger II was a hardtop; it was a showcase for the upcoming production car's radical fastback styling. Except for the absence of wing windows, the roofline was nearly identical to the '66 street car. Also, with one look at the interior you would see virtually the same four-bucket seat office that would arrive in the production car.

The major differences were a stretched rear quarter area and exposed rectangular headlights in a grille with horizontal bars instead of the hideaways set in a vertical motif. According to an article in the February 1965 issue of *Car Craft* magazine, "This one-of-a-kind special has a sleek, ultra-modern appearance but not a 'way out,' car-of-the-future design. In fact some of the features are so utilitarian it might well be a car of tomorrow."

Which, of course, it was.

And there were other Charger show cars as the decade wore on. For 1968 Chrysler rolled out the Charger III, which bore an uncanny resemblance to Chevrolet's '65 Mako Shark II and the production model '68 Corvette. But the ultimate was the '70 Dodge Super Charger. Based on the '68 Topless Charger idea car, this vehicle was updated with a Plymouth Superbird–style nose cone, wore brilliant (and original) Fire Orange paint with a black hood, had a cut-down 10-inch windshield, and, unlike many of its show-only cousins, came equipped with an honest-to-goodness 440-cubic-inch, 375-horse Magnum V8.

Features that never made it to the production line included a rear spoiler that automatically adjusted as speeds increased, vacuum-operated hood vents, side pipes, and twin flip-open gas caps.

The '70 Dodge Super Charger show car (two views, top and above) had its roots in the '68 Topless Charger. Unlike most dream cars, it escaped death at the hands of a car crusher and is today in private hands. Until recently, in fact, it could be seen regularly cruising California's Pacific Coast Highway.

Traveling with the Super Charger that year was another updated beauty from 1969: the Diamante. This car sprang from the Yellowjacket, which was a two-seat Challenger with a lift-off targa top. Its purpose was to showcase the forthcoming '70 Dodge ponycar.

For the 1970 show season, the Diamante, which sported Hemi power (with a 4-speed transmission and 4.10 gears), was given a front fascia with hideaway headlights and a Honey Gold Pearlescent over a yellow base. Its taillights previewed those that would appear on the '72 production Challenger.

Unlike most dream cars, the Dodge Diamante was capable of moving quite briskly under its own power, thanks to a Hemi engine, a 4-speed transmission, and 4.10:1 gears.

Camaro Forerunner

Less fortunate than the Corvette or the Charger II was the Chevrolet Super Nova of 1964. This car was based on a Chevy II platform, but did a fine job of masking that car's plebeian heritage. Unveiled at the New York Auto Show in 1964, it looked very Italian. It is rumored that Bunkie Knudsen, who by this time was working with Chevrolet, was extremely interested in producing it. The Super Nova would have made an exciting Mustang fighter, but Knudsen's hopes were crushed by other GM executives.

This setback was only temporary. As luck would have it, the Super Nova appeared at almost the same time the '65 Ford Mustang was causing sensations in showrooms across the nation. It was the success of its Dearborn rival that would cause Chevrolet to produce the Camaro in 1967. And truth be told, Chevy's ponycar bore more than a passing resemblance to the Super Nova.

There were a host of other remarkable Chevrolet dream cars in the early sixties; most were variations on the Corvette and the econo-minded Corvair. Starting with the '61 Mako Shark show car, Chevy started a trend of providing an uncanny glimpse into future production Corvettes with its show jobs—the basic shape of the '63 Corvette Sting Ray body could be seen in the Mako Shark.

Chevrolet started teasing the public about the upcoming '63 Corvette Sting Ray (above) when it released the Mako Shark I show car (top) in 1961. The Mako Shark I shared many of its body lines with Bill Mitchell's Stingray race car.

While considered a wild design, the '68 Corvette (above) was actually toned down quite a bit from the vehicle on which it was based: the Mako Shark II show car (opposite), which had a fastback roofline with bad blind spots and high, arching front fenders that greatly hindered forward visibility.

Similarly, the Mako Shark II and the '68 Vette were more alike than anyone could have imagined. In fact, had it not been for poor visibility caused by the high, arching fenders and the terrible aerodynamics of the dream car, the production car would have been a near twin.

Larry Shinoda, the man responsible for much of the Corvette's styling during the sixties, also designed a number of Corvair dream cars. Most of these vehicles were based on two-seat designs that, coupled with the Corvair's rear-engine configuration, would have made for outstanding, low-priced entry sports cars. The '64 Monza GT coupe and the '66 Monza SS, in particular, could be introduced today and they would still look modern. And they would probably also sell very well.

For fans of the big Chevrolets, the '65 Concour was one of the prettiest. Based on a two-door Impala convertible, it had shaved door handles, hideaway headlights, and new-for-'65 396 Rat power. It was superseded in 1966 by the Caribe, a breathtaking four-door convertible.

Banshee Blues

While the Camaro could trace its roots to the Super Nova, the Firebird had a different tale to tell. Its name dated back to the jet fighter–shaped Pontiac show car of the '54 Motorama, a car that reappeared in 1956 as the Firebird II and again in 1958. During the sixties, John DeLorean wanted no part of the ponycar concept. He was convinced that a low-priced, two-place sports car was the

way to go. Not a Corvette fighter, but a smaller, more economical sportster—a concept that would finally bear fruit in 1984 with the Pontiac Fiero.

In 1963 DeLorean had two running prototypes built. Both called the Banshee, these cars appeared in 1964. One was a 6-cylinder coupe, the other a V8-propelled roadster. Both were beautiful and were designed to keep costs under $2,500. While there were other cars, including the '66 Banshee, that bore this nameplate, this car simply wasn't destined to become a production vehicle. This was one time when the brash, young DeLorean was completely off the mark. A sporty four-seater had an infinitely broader appeal than a two-seater.

That didn't mean, however, that Pontiac was finished with two-seat concept cars. In fact, the first Fiero was a 1969 Firebird-based showstopper. Like the production 'Bird, it rode on a 108-inch wheelbase. Power came from a high-output version of the 400. The styling bore the traditional Pontiac split bumper, but there was a strange resemblance to Corvettes of the mid-sixties.

Two more Banshee dream machines would surface in the seventies. The first was based on the '73–'74 Super Duty Trans Am, complete with the staggering 455 engine and Turbo 400 transmission; the second was an updated version of the first with different wheels and taillights. At a glance, the profiles of both were very similar to the '75 Chevrolet Monza 2+2 and Pontiac Sunbird. Both also used the "window within a window" side glass that would later appear on the Lamborghini Countach, the Subaru SVX sport coupe, and DeLorean's own DMC-12 exotic car.

Ponycar Concepts

As the sixties wore on and more and more money was invested in the ponycar market, it was only natural that many of the show cars would be based on these platforms. American Motors tested the waters with its original American Motors Experimental (AMX), which was unveiled at the New York Auto Show in June 1966. The AMX was unlike anything that had ever been hatched by the tiny automaker. Onlookers stared in disbelief at its sleek shape, side pipes, and rumble seat. It bore a striking resemblance to the upcoming '68 Javelin, and Robert Evans, the new chairman of AMC, gave it the go-ahead for production.

Chevrolet has shown a wide array of Camaro concepts to the public over the past thirty or so years, including some beauties when the model was in its infancy. The first was the Waikiki Camaro, a convertible for the surfer crowd. Its sides were adorned with fake wood paneling, its tubular grille had rectangular headlamps, and it rode on spoke wheels. Naturally, it had a rack for your surfboard.

As the decade was coming to a close, Chevy attached the Caribe name to a Camaro. Like many dream cars of the era, this one had a targa top.

Top: The operational 1966 AMX dream car by Vignale, which had a functioning rumble seat. Above and left: Two 1966 AMX design sketches by members of AMC's styling staff. The one at left, by Erich Kugler, hints at the production roofline. The one above, by Harold Krispinsky, bears no resemblance to the actual production car.

While the muscle car era was all but dead, Chevrolet tantalized the public with mid-engine concept Corvettes, like the Aerovette, which sported a 400-cube small block. Originally, the Aerovette was called the 4-Rotor because of it Rotary power plant.

But instead of a backseat, the Caribe's roof swept back into a pickup truck bed, à la the El Camino. Another favorite was the Kammback, a sporty wagon based on the second-generation Camaro, which hearkened back to the Corvette Nomad wagon from the '54 Motorama. (Pontiac would also tease the public with a handful of Firebird wagons over the next two decades.)

Ford dabbled with a couple more versions of the Mustang, but the most telling of all wasn't actually a 'Stang. It was called the Bearcat and it resembled the J-car, Ford's second-generation LeMans racer. Based on a 104-inch wheelbase, it had the flatback roof styling that later appeared on the '71 Mustang Mach 1.

As the muscle car era came to a close, Chevrolet tantalized the public with thrilling mid-engine Corvette-based show cars like the Reynolds aluminum 'Vette and the 4-Rotor (later renamed the Aerovette), which remains perhaps the most beautiful Corvette ever. But it was AMC, oddly enough, that shocked showgoers with two mid-engine designs of its own.

The first of the mid-engine specials was the AMX/2, a two-seater designed by staff members of the in-house studio headed by the late Dick Teague and introduced at the Chicago Auto Show in February 1969. However, it was the revised version of this vehicle—the AMX/3—that blew people's doors off.

Powered by a midship-mounted, 340-horse 390, the AMX/3 debuted in Europe and was introduced to the home market on April 4, 1970, at the International Auto Show in New York. American Motors planned a production run of twenty-four cars per year, but federal regulations and cost overruns killed the program after five (or possibly six) cars were built. AMC ordered these cars destroyed, but some escaped the crusher and every once in a while one will turn up for sale.

As tough as it was to take, many of these custom dream cars suffered the same fate planned for the AMX/3s. Most were updated once or twice, then scrapped. Fortunately, this was not always the case, and some of the finest have survived.

Metric Conversions

Because the specifications and measurements of American cars built during this period were measured according to the imperial system of measures, no metric conversions are given within the book. For those interested in the metric equivalents of measurements provided in this book, here is a handy conversion chart.

IMPERIAL MEASURE	METRIC EQUIVALENT
Length	
1 inch	2.54 centimetres
1 foot	0.31 metres
1 mile	1.61 kilometres
Volume	
1 cubic inch	16.39 cubic centimetres
1 gallon	3.79 litres
Speed	
1 mile per hour	1.61 kilometres per hour
Weight	
1 pound	0.45 kilograms
1 ton	907.18 kilograms

Automobile Associations and Clubs

UNITED STATES

All Marques
National Muscle Car Association
3402 Democrat Road
Memphis, TN 38118

Specialty
Hurst/Olds Club of America
1600 Knight Road
Ann Arbor, MI 48103

American Motors
American Motor Owners Association
517 New Hampshire
Portage, MI 49081

National American Motors Drivers & Racers
    Association
P.O. Box 987
Twin Lakes, WI 53181

Chrysler Corporation
Mopar Muscle Club International
879 Summerlea Avenue
Washington, PA 15301

National Hemi Owners Association
1693 S. Reese Road
Reese, MI 48757

Plymouth Barracuda/'Cuda Owners Club
4825 Indian Trail Road
Northampton, PA 18067

Ford Motor Company
Cougar Club of America
18660 Rivercliff Park
Fairview Park, OH 44126

International Mercury Owners Association
6445 West Grand Avenue
Chicago, IL 60635

Mustang Club of America
P.O. Box 447
Lithonia, GA 30058

Performance Ford Club of America
13155 U.S. Route 23
Ashville, OH 43103

Shelby American Automobile Club
P.O. Box 788
Sharon, CT 06069

General Motors
Buick Gran Sport Club of America
1213 Gornto Road
Valdosta, GA 31602

Buick Motor Division
Buick Club of America
P.O. Box 898
Garden Grove, CA 92642

Chevrolet Motor Division
COPO Connection
P.O. Box 1036
Lombard, IL 60148

International Camaro Club, Inc.
2001 Pittstown Avenue
Scranton, PA 18505

National Chevelle Owners Association
7343-J West Friendly Avenue
Greensboro, NC 27410

National Corvettes Restorers Society
6291 Day Road
Cincinnati, OH 45252

National Council of Corvette Clubs
Route 1, Box 373
High Springs, FL 32643

National Monte Carlo Owners Association
P.O. Box 187
Independence, KY 41051

Oldsmobile Motor Division
Oldsmobile Club of America
P.O. Box 16216
Lansing, MI 48901

Pontiac Motor Division
GTO Association of America
1634 Briarson Drive
Saginaw, MI 48603

Pontiac-Oakland Club International
P.O. Box 4789
Culver City, CA 90230

Trans Am Club of America
P.O. Box 99
Tufts University Bridge
Medford, MA 02153

CANADA

American Motors
Classic AMX Club of Canada
18 Trewartha Crescent
Brampton, Ontario L6Z 1X4

Northern Ramblers
R.R. 3, Maple Grove Road North
Bowmanville, Ontario L1C 3K4

Chrysler Corporation
Maritime Mopar Musclecar Association
265 Old Sachville
Sachville, Nova Scotia B4C 2J5

Mopar Performance Group
3 Skegby Road
Brampton, Ontario L6V 2T8

Motivated Mopars Car Club
P.O. Box 1147
Cobourg, Ontario K9A 5A4

Vancouver Mopar Club
5023 Gladstone Street
Vancouver, British Columbia V5P 4C1

Ford Motor Company
Alberta Mustang Owners Association
P.O. Box 6567
Station C
Edmonton, Alberta T5B 4M4

Central Alberta Classic Ford Club
P.O. Box 1008
Red Deer, Alberta T4N 6S5

Greater Vancouver Mustang Association
P.O. Box 69124
Vancouver, British Columbia V5K 4W4

Ontario Mustang Club
312 Lancaster Street West
Kitchener, Ontario N2H 4V7

General Motors
Buick Motor Division
Buick Gran Sport Club of America, British
    Columbia Chapter
101 Battleford Avenue
Victoria, British Columbia V8Z 1K6

Chevrolet Motor Division
Toronto Classic Chevy Unlimited
9 Campertown Avenue
Toronto, Ontario M9R 3T3

Classic GTO Club of Ontario
630 Bloor Street East
Oshawa, Ontario L1H 3N2

Oldsmobile Motor Division
Olds 4-4-2/Cutlass Club
11 Lambeth Square
Toronto, Ontario M1W 3B3

Pontiac Motor Division
British Columbia Trans Am Association
2942 West 19th Avenue
Vancouver, British Columbia V6L 1E6

ENGLAND

American Auto Club NW
276 Greenside Lane
Droylsgen, Manchester M43 7SL

American Motor Club UK
20 Fort Royal Hill
Worcester WR5 1BT

Photo Credits

1963 CORVETTE STING RAY Z06

INDEX